FEARSO

PASSAGES

A personal exploration of some infamous waters

David Rainsbury

IMRAY LAURIE NORIE & WILSON

Published by
Imray Laurie Norie & Wilson Ltd
Wych House The Broadway
St Ives Cambridgeshire PE27 5BT England
☎ +44(0)1480 462114
Fax +44(0)1480 496109
www.imray.com
2005

1st edition 2005

A catalogue record for this book is available from the British Library.

ISBN 0 85288 836 8

CAUTION

Every effort has been made to ensure the accuracy of this book. It contains selected information and thus is not definitive and does not include all known information on the subject in hand; this is particularly relevant to the plans, which should not be used for navigation. The author believes that his selection is a useful aid to prudent navigation, but the safety of a vessel depends ultimately on the judgement of the navigator, who should assess all information, published or unpublished.

PLANS

The plans in this guide are not to be used for navigation. They are designed to support the text and should at all times be used with navigational charts.

Printed in Italy by Eurolitho SpA, Milan

CONTENTS

SCOTLAND

Fort William

Loch Linnhe
Mull
8 Oban
Jura Crinan
Islay GLASGOW
Kintyre Arran
Rathlin Firth of Clyde 11
Larne Stranraer
BELFAST
15 North Channel
Isle of Man

IRELAND Irish Sea

DUBLIN 5 Anglesey
4 16
2 Pwllheli
Cardigan Bay WALES ENGLAND

St George's Channel
Fishguard
9 Tenby Swansea
CARDIFF 3 BRISTOL
Bristol Channel

Barnstaple Southampton
Poole 10 Chichester
Needles 7
13 Bill of Portland Isle of Wight

Lands End Start Pt English Channel

Alderney
1 CHERBOURG
Guernsey

Jersey

12 Orfordness
Harwich

Dover Strait

FRANCE

Ouessant BREST
6 Morgat Brittany
14 Audierne

Bay of Biscay

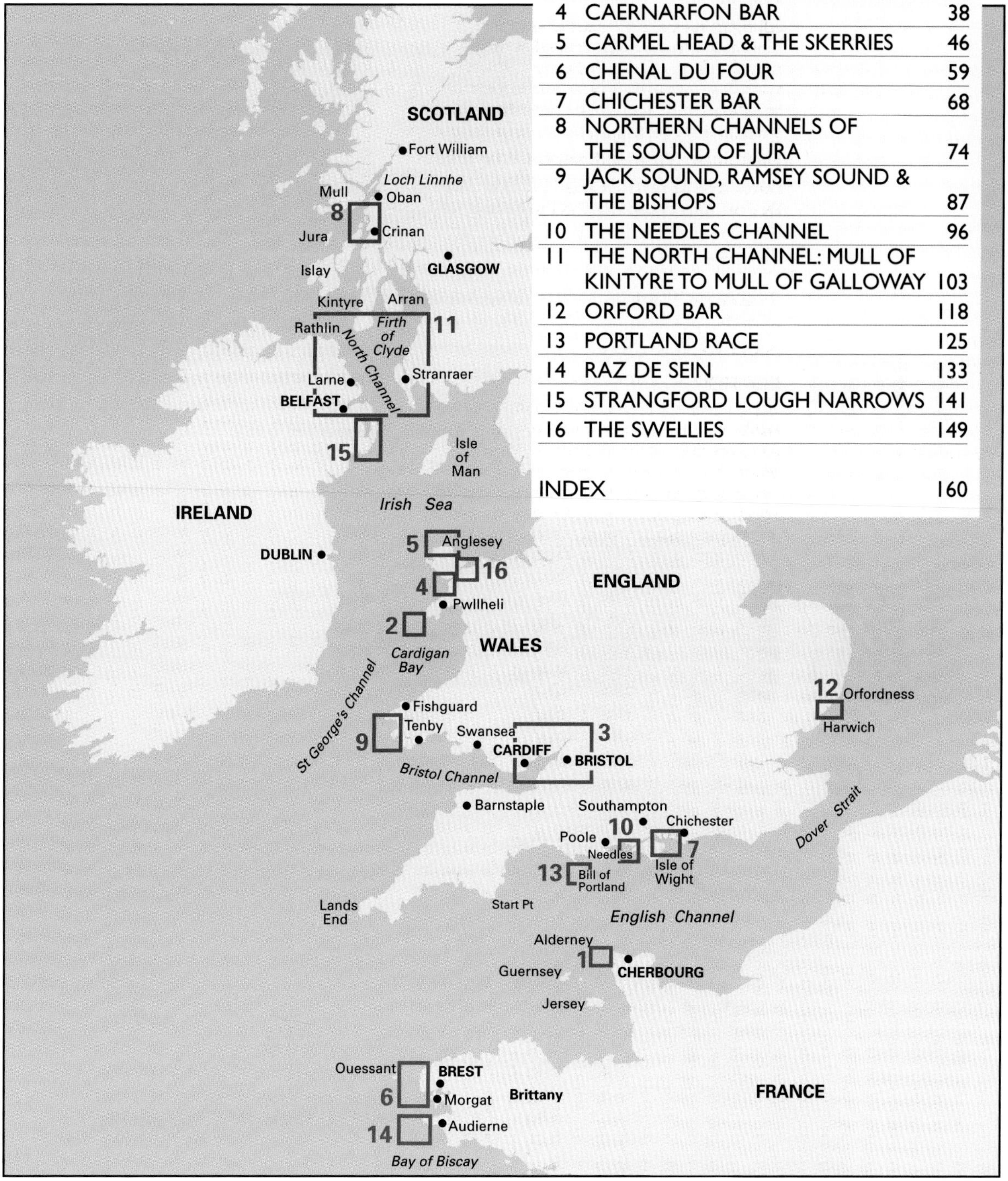

PREFACE

There are many stretches of water that have fearsome reputations among cruising sailors, some more deserved than others. Many skippers will have one point on a cruise that they will be glad to have behind them, a headland or narrows that haunts their dreams and has them poring over charts and tidal atlas days in advance to check and double check the timing, memorising courses and transits and the positions of rocks. There is the potential for disaster in each of the passages but these are also waters that yachts and small boats routinely pass through, the vast majority without drama or incident. The key without exception is to choose the right time and favourable conditions.

The Fearsome Passages in these pages are ones that have kept me awake at night, rehearsing the horror stories of the yacht club bar and the dire warnings of pilot books. I have sailed through all of them, mostly singlehanded aboard *Piper*, my little Contessa 26. A faithful friend and a brave little ship, she has kept going when I wanted to quit and has carried me from the fjords of Norway to the warmth of the Loire and right around Britain and Ireland. When, in describing my own experience I say 'we', I generally mean me and *Piper*.

I have made many mistakes in making these Fearsome Passages but so far have lived to tell the tale. In sharing *Piper's* experience I have owned up to some of them and have tried to learn how to do things better next time. The sea can be an unforgiving critic.

David Rainsbury
High Peak
June 2005

ABOUT THE AUTHOR

David Rainsbury has been sailing for over 25 years, mostly from his base in the Irish Sea. Beginning with a Hurley 22 which he sailed on the shallows of the River Dee, he has sailed the waters of Britain, Ireland and Western Europe from Norway to Gibraltar, with forays into the Med and the Caribbean. Though an Ocean Yachtmaster he prefers coastal and offshore cruising and tends to head north rather than south. His latest yacht, *Piper*, is a Contessa 26 built by Jeremy Rogers in 1969.

David is a freelance photographer and writer and uses his sailing as the raw material for his work.

For Kathy

1. ALDERNEY RACE AND THE SWINGE

The island of Alderney, the northernmost of the Channel Islands, sits at the northwest corner of the Cotentin Peninsula. The Channel Islands have one of the biggest tidal ranges anywhere in the world, in excess of 10 metres at springs. The currents that flow around this exposed corner of France sweep through the gap between Alderney and the mainland and between the islands themselves, making this a notorious area of sea, dangerous for the unwary or ill-prepared to venture into.

'Alderney is all about tidal streams. It sits off one of the most tide-swept of all headlands, and the race between this and the island is of international notoriety.'

Tom Cunliffe
Shell Channel Pilot

The broad stretch of water between Cap de la Hague and Alderney is the formidable Alderney Race. The strong

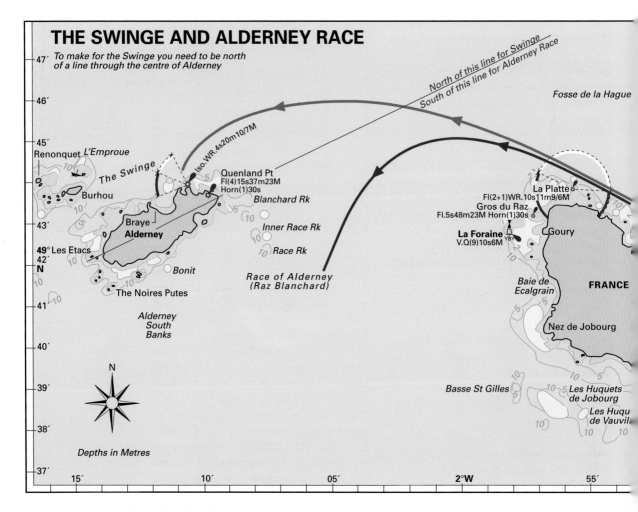

THE SWINGE AND ALDERNEY RACE

currents and turbulence are generated by the enormous volume of water that pours in from the wider part of the Channel as the sea around the Channel Islands makes its dramatic changes in tidal level. Between Alderney and the small island of Burhou water passing to the north of Alderney squeezes between rock-strewn shores over an uneven bottom at rates in excess of 6kn. This is the Swinge.

MAKING THE CHOICE

On passage between the Channel Islands and Cherbourg or the English coast you have the choice of going through the Alderney Race or of going around the small island of Alderney and into the Swinge. A third option is to head further west, through the Ortac Channel between the Casquets and Alderney, but this will not avoid the difficulties altogether. The tides remain strong and in your path lie the reefs and shoals of the Casquet Bank.

From the north

Coming from the south coast of England the most popular option for cruising yachts is to cross to the port of Cherbourg, using its excellent sheltered harbour as a jumping-off point for venturing around Cap de la Hague into the strong tides of Channel Island waters. It is important to choose your course carefully when approaching from the north. The tidal streams may decide your destination for you if you are not in the right place at the right time. Streams divide around Alderney, roughly on a line through the long axis of the island. Get north of this line to go to Braye or the Swinge, south of this line to go through Alderney Race.

If you are in a hurry and conditions are right the Alderney Race gives the fastest access to the South. Making for St Peter Port or Jersey it is best to arrive at

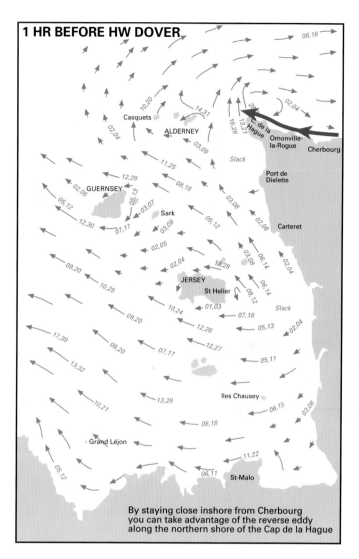

By staying close inshore from Cherbourg you can take advantage of the reverse eddy along the northern shore of the Cap de la Hague

Cap de la Hague at high water. By staying close inshore between Cherbourg and the Cap de la Hague a yacht can take advantage of a reverse eddy which will give a lift to the west, rather than facing a foul tide farther off. Arriving at the Cap at slack water, just before the tide begins to run southwards, will give a *relatively* gentle ride through the Alderney Race and a fast passage towards the Little Russel and St Peter Port or down to Jersey. Conditions to avoid are, of course, wind over tide. With any wind from the southwest the Alderney Race is not the place to be. Better in that case to stay

La Foraine West cardinal and Cap de La Hague lighthouse

well to the north and head for Alderney, or go back to Cherbourg or the little harbour of Omonville la Rogue, just 3M east of the Cap de la Hague.

Alderney is my favourite of the Channel Islands so I never miss a chance to visit, timing a passage from Cherbourg to arrive on the last of the ebb. This means staying well to the north of Cap de la Hague and north of the line through the centre of Alderney.

The Swinge can be very nasty, with steep breaking seas building up very quickly and in fairly confined waters from slack water rates attaining almost five knots within an hour after the turn and a maximum spring rate of 6.8kn in the middle of the tide. However, the area of rough water is not so extensive as in the Alderney Race and by judicious timing the roughest conditions can be avoided altogether. Stephen Shaw is Braye Harbourmaster and for 18 years was cox'n of Alderney Lifeboat, during which time he was involved in the saving of 325 lives.

'The key is to use the tides. If you go at slack water you won't get into the overfalls because they're not there.'

Slack water lasts only a short time, occurring at +0500 Dover at low water and –0100 Dover at high water, the flood running northeast.

The worst of the overfalls in the Swinge form on the downtide side of a ledge running from Corbet Rock on the Alderney side to North Rock on the Burhou side of the Swinge, which has a depth of 3.4 metres over it at LAT. A yacht on passage southward via the Swinge would normally call in at Braye, stopping short of the overfalls. From here the timing of slack water is simple and, if in any doubt as to conditions outside, a look at the Swinge from the breakwater can help in making a decision.

From the south

Timing is more of a problem when making for Braye from the south, as the strength of the tide will have the unwary

THE ALDERNEY RACE

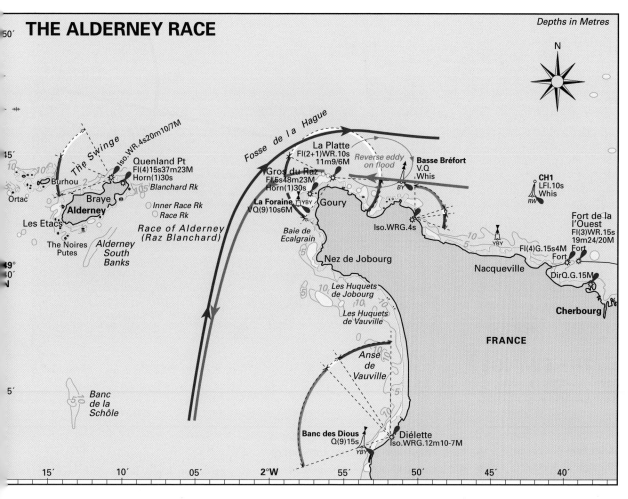

Depths in Metres

N

50'

The Swinge

Iso.WR.4s20m10/7M

Quenland Pt
Fl(4)15s37m23M
Horn(1)30s

Burhou

Blanchard Rk

Ortac

Braye

Inner Race Rk

Race Rk

Alderney

15'

Les Etacs

Race of Alderney
(Raz Blanchard)

The Noires
Putes

Alderney
South
Banks

49°
40'
N

5'

Banc
de la
Schôle

Fosse de la Hague

La Platte
Fl(2+1)WR.10s
11m9/6M

Reverse eddy
on flood

Basse Bréfort
V.Q
Whis

Gros du Raz
Fl.5s48m23M
Horn(1)30s

BY

CH1
LFl.10s
Whis

RW

La Foraine
VQ(9)10s6M

YBY

Goury

Iso.WRG.4s

Fort de la
l'Ouest
Fl(3)WR.15s
19m24/20M

Baie de
Ecalgrain

Nez de Jobourg

YBY

Fl(4)G.15s4M

Fort

Fort

Nacqueville

DirQ.G.15M

Les Huquets
de Jobourg

Cherbourg

Les Huquets
de Vauville

FRANCE

Anse
de
Vauville

Banc des Dious
Q(9)15s

YBY

Diélette
Iso.WRG.12m10-7M

15'   10'   05'   2°W   55'   50'   45'   40'

into the Swinge far earlier than expected. To cut it too fine could well result in the tide turning foul before you are safely through. The ideal timing is to arrive at the Swinge with just enough north-going tide to carry you up to Braye. Such is the strength of the tide and the difference between spring and neap rates that this calculation can be difficult to get right. On the flood the worst of the overfalls form towards the Burhou shore and northeast of a line between Corbet Rock and Burhou. By staying close to the Alderney shore the worst of the rough water can be avoided. Unfortunately, the Alderney shore is littered with rocks and shoals so careful pilotage is called for.

PILOTAGE

Alderney Race

Pilotage of the Alderney Race is essentially simple. It is a wide stretch of water, clear of hazards in the main part of the channel, except for the strength of the tide. To make a safe passage of the Race and end up at your intended destination, the key is timing.

The tidal diamonds on the chart record rates up to 6 knots but an examination of the Admiralty *Tidal Stream Atlas* reveals rates well in excess of this, in reality over eight knots.

Coming from Cherbourg, it is possible by staying close inshore to make use of

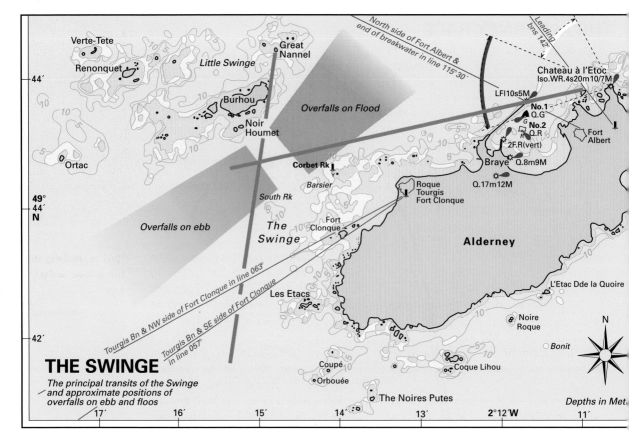

THE SWINGE

*The principal transits of the Swinge
and approximate positions of
overfalls on ebb and floos*

Great Nannel shows to the right of Burhou. This transit (009°) clears the shoals to the south and west of Alderney and avoids the Pierre au Vraic in the southern approach to the Swinge

the back eddy on the north side of Cap de la Hague and arrive off the Cap at slack water. Then stand out into open water before rounding so as to avoid the rough stuff inshore. The greatest risk with the Alderney Race is an encounter with wind against the tide when seas can be steep enough to overwhelm a yacht. In conditions of favourable wind and tide the seas can be steep but are generally

manageable. The worst overfalls develop downtide of Race Rock and over the Alderney South Banks, also close inshore off the Cap de la Hague where streams can attain up to 10kn. The smoothest water will be found midway between Alderney and Cap de la Hague.

The Swinge

The smoothest water is to be found on the Alderney side of the passage. Unfortunately, the Alderney shore is littered with awash rocks which extend some way out into the Swinge. For this reason many yachts keep a respectful distance, staying over to the Burhou side, and so encounter the rougher conditions. There is much more space in the Swinge than the impression one gets from the chart, and careful use of clearing bearings and transits a yacht can safely avoid the roughest water and stay clear of the rocks.

The two principal transits are marked on Admiralty chart 60:

'Great Nannel with the eastern edge of the rocky shore of Burhou clears the shoals to the south and west of Alderney (009°). This transit also avoids the Pierre au Vraic in the southern approach to the Swinge.

The transit of the outer end of the breakwater with the Chateau à l'Etoc light (080°) will clear Corbet Rock.'

Adhering closely to these transits will take a yacht over towards the Burhou shore and into the overfalls on that side. A transit of the root of the breakwater and the northern edge of Fort Albert (083°) marks the extent of the rocks, enabling a yacht to creep closer inshore until north of the Rogue Tourgis Fort. East of here Les Jumelles extend north of this line. Braye harbourmaster Stephen Shaw recommends using a GPS waypoint to clear the Corbet rock.

Braye Harbour

Extending beyond the end of the breakwater at Braye lie the submerged ruins of an extension, destroyed by storms shortly after it was completed. In places there is just over a metre of water at LAT. Approaching from the northeast

this represents no problem when following the leading lights (215°). In daylight the upper mark is sometimes difficult to spot, surrounded by trees on the lane up from the harbour. The church spire is just to the left of this line and is on the skyline in plain view. Coming from the Swinge, leading beacons (142°) clear the ruins. The lower mark is a pole on a rock in Saye Bay; the upper on the hillside beyond is a thin metal tripod.

HARBOURS AND ANCHORAGES

Braye

49°43′.5N 02°12′.00W

Braye harbour has more a feel of the Outer Hebrides than the Channel Islands, having a wilder and more

Piper **approaching the Swinge from St Peter Port**

Quenard light is visible in line with the end of the Braye breakwater

PIPER'S EXPERIENCE ALDERNEY RACE

My first encounter with Alderney Race had been in strong winds aboard the Ocean Youth Trust vessel *Master Builder*. I was on galley duty below and each time the 76ft ketch fell off a wave the oven door flew open.

To experience both the Alderney Race and the Swinge in one trip, *Piper* made the passage from Cherbourg down through the Alderney Race to arrive at the Noires Putes for slack water (Dover +0500). We then took the first of the flood up through the Swinge to Braye. Leaving Cherbourg we stood off from Cap de la Hague until about 2 miles west of the lighthouse. The wind was a light northwesterly and the last of the ebb, almost at neaps, carried us swiftly southwards as large rounded seas rose up astern with an eerie rolling motion. South of Race Rock I used a convenient transit ashore to check Piper's course to pass to the north of the South Banks, her heading once as much as 045° up on her track. A clearing bearing off the Quenard lighthouse kept me clear of the Bonit as we passed inside the South Banks on the last of the tide. With Coque Lihou in line with the

tip of Alderney I turned towards the Noires Putes, holding the westerly heading until the Great Nannel and the eastern edge of Burhou were in line. Slack water was very well defined and soon the north-going stream was pushing us up towards Braye. With the wind on *Piper's* beam and the flood still in its infancy, our passage of the Swinge dispelled the foreboding that had haunted my thoughts since we left Cherbourg.

Any passage around the Channel Islands calls for careful calculation of the tides. My introduction to the Swinge was on passage from St Peter Port. I checked my workings several times before *Piper* and I set out for the island of Alderney. The weather was grey and squally and once clear of Guernsey big seas swept in from the west. For all her small size, *Piper* inspires confidence. She gives a wet ride but her motion in a seaway is surefooted, holding well to her windward course. Secured by my harness I sat up to weather on the coachroof, leaving the autohelm to steer as I watched the awesome procession of waves. I could hear the roaring of the breaking water over the Casquet Bank, 3 miles away to the west. I did not want to get nearer.

With the tide under us it was

a fast passage, and sooner than I expected I was lining *Piper* up to enter the Swinge. To port was the rocky islet of Burhou, to starboard the island of Alderney. Between them the Swinge was a heaving mass of curling water as the strength of the flood rushed through. Whatever *Piper's* seakeeping ability, this was not going to be nice. Close in to the Alderney shore the breakers were less severe. Carefully following the transits in the *Channel Islands Pilot* I pressed as close in as possible but one standing wave could not be avoided. Piper rose to it and burst through the crest, drenching the deck sails and crew in a cloud of spray. Hanging for a moment in mid-air she dropped heavily down the other side, and finding calmer water beyond, she flew on toward the Braye harbour entrance.

The approach to Braye harbour from the south is not quite straightforward. The ruins of a failed breakwater extension lie just below the surface and extend some distance from the visible section. I scanned the skyline for the iron beacon, which gives a transit for a safe approach. Spotting it at last I lined *Piper* up, and clear of the hazard rounded up and stowed the sails, securing *Piper* to a visitors' mooring close in the lee of the granite wall.

Stephen Shaw, Braye harbourmaster, was involved in the saving of 325 lives during 18 years as cox'n of Alderney lifeboat.
'The key is to use the tides. If you go at slack water you won't get into the overfalls because they're not there.'

The beacons giving the approach to Braye harbour clear of the ruin of the breakwater extension

The white beacon in line with the church spire is an easier mark to spot in daylight than the leading lights to the right

remote aspect than its genteel neighbours. Ashore, a road runs up to the island's capital of St Anne's where small, neat stone houses line the narrow streets. There is ample evidence of the island's strategic importance through the conflicts that have swept Western Europe, especially the Second World War. Massively built fortifications dominate every approach to the island, commanding clear views of the sea channels and beaches. Many of these were built during the German occupation.

The Channel Islands are not members of the EU so if you have come from France or England you need to clear

A yacht entering the overfalls from Braye against the flood

The upper leading light for the approach to Braye Harbour

Fort Clonque

inward with customs. When you leave, remember when landing in England or France that you are entering the EU from non-EU territory and must clear customs again.

Visitors' moorings are laid inside the breakwater. Fees for using these are collected by harbour staff in their dory or you can visit the harbour office. Showers, toilets and laundry facilities for the use of visiting yachts are at the top of the landing stage steps.

Chandlery and fuel are available in the inner harbour at Mainbrayce Marine who also operate a water taxi between the slip and the moorings.

Contacts

Braye Harbourmaster
☎ 01481 82 2620 VHF Ch 16, 74
Alderney Radio
Mainbrayce Marine ☎ 01481 82 2772

Cherbourg

49°39′.00N 1°37′.00W

Cherbourg is a large bustling town. There are excellent shops and services, an enormous supermarket and good rail connections with Paris. Cherbourg is an attractively cheaper option than berthing a yacht on the south coast of England and with this in mind the ferry company offers discount rates to regular cross-Channel travellers.

The entrances to Cherbourg, whether east or west, are very well lit and marked. From the east, entering via the Passe de l'Est, give a good offing to the Truite Red beacon which marks the northern extremity of Ile Pellée. Leave the Tromet PHM (Fl(4)R.15s) to port and stay towards the western side of the entrance but be aware that debris extends up to 100m from the fort. At night stay in the white sector of the Ft des Flamands (DirQ.RWG). Once past the outer breakwaters a course of 220° will take you to the entrance to the Petite Rade, lit to starboard on the end of the Digue du Homet (Fl.G) and to port with a buoy (VQ.R) off the end of Jetée des Flamands. Thereafter shape a course of 200° for the Port de Chantereyne.

Entering via the Passe de l'Ouest there is a red buoy (Oc.R.4s) just inside the entrance. You must leave this to port. A course of 124° leads you to the end of Digue du Homet and the entrance to the

Petite Rade. At night the light on the Digue du Homet and a light ashore (Iso.G.4s) are the leading lights for this course.

Port de Chantereyne Marina

All the facilities a cruising yacht could require can be found close to the marina. Visitors' berths are on pontoons N, P, Q, on the south side of the marina. Power and water alongside, showers, toilets, weather forecasts at *capitainerie*. An additional pontoon for larger yachts lies in the middle of the fairway. With 300 berths available for visitors the harbour can still get full in busy periods.

Petite Rade

Anchorage may be had to the west of the entrance to Port de Chantereyne in the Petite Rade. Anchor north of the Chantereyne breakwater in 3 to 5 metres, clear of the fairway and the prohibited military area. If things get too lively inside this is a quieter alternative. The free berth in this most popular of harbours also goes some way to offsetting the inconvenience of the dinghy ride. Shelter here is good except in northerlies when there is sufficient fetch to raise a chop.

Avant Port

Additional pontoon berths for visitors have been laid in the Avant Port. You may be directed to berth here if leaving your yacht for some time.

Contacts

Harbourmaster (Port)
☎ 02 33 20 41 25
Marina ☎ 02 33 87 65 70
VHF VTS call *Joburg Traffic* Ch 13, 16
  Marina Call *Chantereyne* Ch 09, 72
  (0800-2300 LT)
  Port Call *Le Homet* Ch 12, 16
Weather information
Cherbourg Detailed forecasts and
  weather maps posted in *capitainerie*.

Tides

Standard port: Cherbourg

Diélette

49°33´.20N 01°51´.70W
Tides
HW St Malo +0040
LW St Malo +0030
Streams
NE begins HW St Malo –0410
SW begins HW St Malo +0135

Diélette is a delightful harbour, recently upgraded to cater for yachts. Just over ten miles from Cap de La Hague it is well placed as a place to wait for conditions to pass the Alderney Race, or to duck into once through from the north. There is a

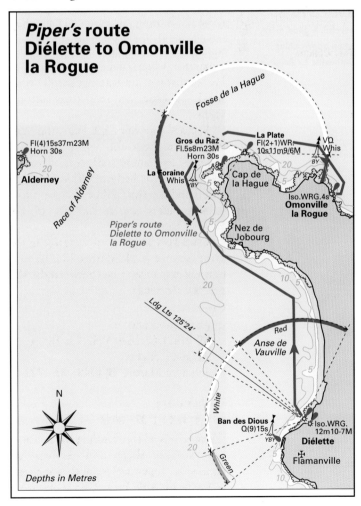

maintained within the marina by a lifting sill. A tide gauge and entry signal lights are to starboard of the sill.

There are few services ashore but the sanitaires block, set by the stream which flows into the harbour, must be one of the prettiest in Northern France. There is a café near the *capitainerie*, two restaurants, one of which is in the yacht club and there is a small hotel in the village up the hill. There are no shops but a small chandlery operates from the same building as the yacht club.

Daily weather forecast printouts are available free of charge at the *capitainerie*.

Basse Brefort N cardinal buoy, with the old semaphore station on the shore beyond. A good mark when approaching Omonville La Rogue

minimum depth of 0.5m in the approach but the Avant Port dries. The Bassin de Commerce is dredged to between 1.5m and 2.5m below chart datum and there is a small waiting pontoon which has enough depth for a yacht to stay afloat, though space is limited as one side is reserved for a ferry service. Water level is

Omonville la Rogue: the sectored light, by day the front transit mark for approach

Omonville la Rogue

49°42´.32N 01°49´.85W

Tides

HW Dover –0330

      Cherbourg –0010

LW Cherbourg –0015

This little harbour is not much more than a roadstead, sheltered from the west by a breakwater. The village is set back from the sea in tranquil green countryside, watched over by its ancient church. The church tower forms the rear leading mark when entering. In the harbour a restaurant and café serve excellent food and there is drinking water from a tap by the Ecole de Voile. Besides being quieter than Cherbourg, Omonville is only 3½ miles from Cap de la Hague.

Before making your approach identify the green unlit beacon on L'Etonnard. The sectored light on the beach is fixed to a white painted gantry. In line with the church this gives a transit clear of all dangers (255°). Both the chart and (in a rare lapse) Tom Cunliffe's Shell Channel Pilot describe the church as having a spire. The church has, in fact, a square tower with a pitched roof. Whatever the architectural detail, the clearest identifying feature from seaward is the large white clock face. At night the white sector of the light gives the approach. Stay in the white sector until you are abeam of L'Etonnard beacon, which should be near enough to starboard to show up in a powerful torch, then turn onto a course of approximately 290°, directly towards the fish restaurant near the root of the pier. The old Customs House mentioned in Reed's is just to the left of this.

The visitors' moorings are laid outside the smaller moorings and are marked by large white conical buoys topped with a stainless steel mooring ring.

FIRING RANGE

ENE of the entrance to Omonville la Rogue is a military firing range. When this is active a red flag is flown from the breakwater head.

CHARTS AND PILOTS

Imray C33A

Admiralty 60, 3653

SHOM 7086, 6966, 7092, 7420

The Shell Channel Pilot Tom Cunliffe (Imray)

North Brittany and the Channel Islands RCC Pilotage Foundation/John Lawson (Imray)

Secret Anchorages of Brittany Peter Cumberlidge (Imray)

Piper alongside the waiting pontoon at Diélette

2. BARDSEY SOUND

The Lleyn Peninsula extends its long arm out into the tides of the Irish Sea. At the extreme end of this arm is Bardsey Island, separated from the mainland by Bardsey Sound, a mile of swirling water that gave Bardsey its Welsh name Ynys Enlli, the Island of Eddies. Seeking sanctuary from the trials of Dark Age Britain, monks found refuge on Bardsey Island, earning the island another title, 'The isle of 20,000 saints'. Here they set up their communities protected by the turbulent waters of Bardsey Sound. The ruins of a 13th century Abbey still stand on the island.

Facing the island across the sound is the Bay delightfully named Hell's Mouth.

In a southwesterly gale this bay can live up to its name.

Yachts passing between Cardigan Bay and harbours further north have the option of going around the island, an extra two hours with a fair wind, or of braving Bardsey Sound. Tides running at two knots or more in the rest of the Irish Sea are constricted by the Lleyn Peninsula and accelerate as the mass of water is pushed westwards to join the main body of water in the Irish Sea. At Bardsey Sound the flow is further compressed as the water is forced between the island and the Lleyn Peninsula, and with rates attaining 6kn at springs conditions can get very rough.

Bardsey Island from the south

BARDSEY SOUND

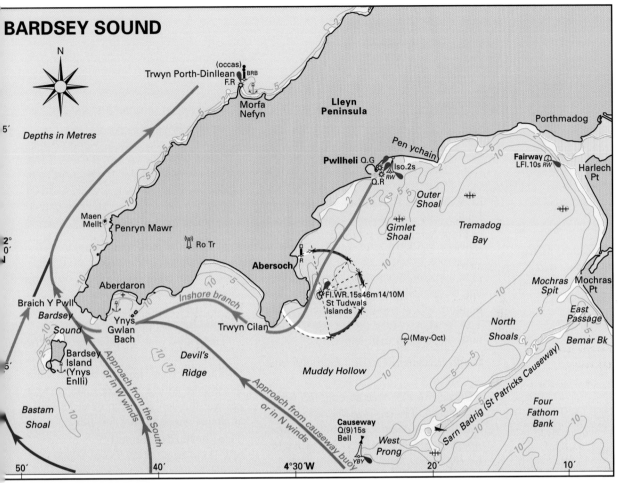

With wind over tide, standing waves of prodigious heights have been experienced.

'Bardsey Sound can be evil – 50-foot standing waves have been reported but thankfully never experienced. Only tackle it in fair weather and at slack water.'

Ralph Morris
Cruising Anglesey and Adjacent Waters (NWVYC)

Within the sound the roughest water occurs at the northern end on the flood and at the southern end on the ebb. A back eddy can form very close inshore on the mainland side, setting in two hours before the turn of the tide. With local knowledge this can be used to sneak through against the flow in calm conditions.

On the flood the roughest water is to be found to the north of Bardsey. Around the rocks close to the north side of the tip of the Lleyn at Braich y Pwll is the reef known as the Tripods which kicks up some nasty seas. Another area of overfalls forms to the north of Bardsey Island and the drying rock Maen Bugail. At times this extends well out into the track that would be followed if sticking to the middle of the sound.

Several areas of overfalls occur to the south and west of the island on both flood and ebb. Bastram Shoal is a ridge due south of Bardsey that rises to a depth of just over 6m. The Devil's Ridge is a similar shoal almost in line with Bardsey

Sound. Both of these can produce dangerous breaking seas in strong wind over tide conditions. The Devil's Tail is a line of overfalls which extends ten miles or more to the south of Bardsey Sound. This is at its worst on the ebb and is more unpleasant than dangerous.

Local yachtsman Derek Lumb has this advice:

'Whenever we've been through it's been a pussy-cat. The secret is the right time and the right conditions. Leaving from Aberdaron or even Abersoch it's easy to get the timing right. The horror stories we've heard have been from crews approaching from a distance and getting it wrong.'

For vessels making a direct crossing of Cardigan Bay from the south the hump of Bardsey Island appears over the horizon to the west of the hills of the Lleyn Peninsula from fifteen or more miles away. From the sand dunes of Abermenai at the southeastern entrance to the Menai Strait the mountains of the Lleyn appear to have much greater height than they possess, marching down toward the horizon in a series of mounds and peaks. Bardsey is visible as the final summit. If making for Holyhead from the Bishops, Bardsey Sound gives no advantage: the direct course passes offshore of the island, but for a passage to or from the bays on either side of the Lleyn Peninsula the passage of Bardsey Sound can save time, not only by shortening the distance over the ground but by the extraordinary burst of speed donated by the tide.

The safest time to pass through the sound is at slack water, just as the tide is turning in your favour, but in calm weather or with a moderate fair wind a passage through the sound can be made at almost any state of a fair tide.

Tides in Bardsey Sound
NW flood begins HW Dover +0500
SE ebb begins HW Dover −0100

NORTHWARD PASSAGE

The northern half of Cardigan Bay is fraught with dangers. St Patrick's Causeway extends out into the bay for nearly fourteen miles and is awash for much of its length, drying in places to just over a metre. It is marked at its western end by the Causeway W cardinal buoy. Passing northward towards Caernarfon Bar or Holyhead it is helpful to have enough fair tide once through the sound to carry you over the Bar or around the Stacks. Some careful passage-planning is required if your departure point is well to the south and will mean facing a strong contrary stream to arrive at the sound early in the flood.

Alternatively, anchorage can be found in several places in which to wait out a foul tide. Henllwyn Cove on Bardsey Island and Aberdaron on the Lleyn are the closest to the sound but the protection offered is far from complete. Abersoch and Pwllheli in Tremadoc Bay have the better shelter but are about two hours away from the entrance to the Sound.

To arrive at Bardsey Sound from Tremadoc Bay pass inshore of St Tudwal's Isle. The reverse eddy within the sound extends as far as Trwyn Cilan. To take advantage of this, time your departure to arrive in St Tudwal's Sound up to 2 hours before Bardsey slack. From Trwyn Cilan stay close inshore across Hell's Mouth and pass inshore of Ynys Gwlan Fawr into Aberdaron Bay.

Approaching directly from the south pass between the Bastram Shoal and The Devil's Ridge. From the Causeway buoy the Devil's Ridge is directly in your way. If the wind is from the north the preferred track is under the lee of the Lleyn as from Tremadoc Bay. In westerly winds a track outside the Devil's Ridge will avoid overfalls off the headland at Pen y Cil and give a freer sail through the sound.

In the sound hold a northwesterly track until well clear and give The Tripods and Braich y Pwll a good offing before turning into Caernarfon Bay.

SOUTHWARD PASSAGE

Porth Dinllaen is an excellent departure point for a passage through the sound. Leave an hour before high water and run parallel to the shore, standing out to clear the Tripods. The worst water is on the southeastern end of the sound, in line with the Devil's Ridge. If heading directly south keep rather more to the island side of the sound once past Maen Bugail. For the Causeway buoy or Tremadoc Bay: once Aberdaron Bay is open, shape a course for Ynys Gwlan Bach to avoid

Bardsey ight from Henllwyn Cove, with seals basking on the rocky shore

being set down into the broken water of the Devil's Ridge.

GOING OUTSIDE

If fresh to strong winds are expected, especially against the tide, Bardsey Sound is to be avoided. The seas in these conditions are savage enough to cause structural damage to a well built yacht. For a passage around the outside give an offing of at least three or four miles to Bardsey Island, the Bastram shoal and the end of the Lleyn. Once in Caernarfon Bay the nearest shelter northwards is some distance away. Porth Dinllaen is not ideal in northerly winds so Llanddwyn Island, over twenty miles away at the entrance to Caernarfon Bar, is the next alternative. An early decision to seek shelter in Tremadoc Bay could save heartache later. Faced with southerly winds on a southbound passage, the Bastram shoal must be cleared before turning in toward any haven in Cardigan Bay or Tremadoc Bay.

Bardsey light indicates the position of Henllwyn Cove from the southern end of Bardsey Sound

Seals basking on the rocky shore of Henllwyn Cove

Approaching Henllwyn Cove from the Sound

HARBOURS AND ANCHORAGES

Henllwyn Cove

52°45′.0N 04°47′.6W

Henllwyn Cove is on the southeast of Bardsey Island. In settled weather this is an exquisite anchorage, well sheltered from the west. Holding is rather poor due to the weed but the rocky shore is alive with seals basking, often popping up beside a yacht for a closer look at the visitors. Approach the anchorage on a westerly track on the centre line of the cove, keeping a careful watch for submerged rocks. Landing on the island is not encouraged but is allowed if visitors give due regard to wildlife and farming needs.

Aberdaron Bay

52°47′.8N 04°43′.1W

Aberdaron Bay can be approached from eastwards if conditions demand it, passing between Ynys Gwlan Fawr and the mainland. The bay offers no protection from southerly quarters but is very convenient for Bardsey Sound. Ashore there is a pub and shop.

Abersoch

52°49´.5N 04°28´.0W

HW Dover –0315

Though farther from Bardsey Sound, the bay is sheltered from all quarters except east. Visitors' moorings may be available off the yacht club or anchor clear of the moorings. A sewage outfall extends ENE from Penbennar. Its end, marked by a perch, is at the springs low-water mark. Showers and water are available at the yacht club. This is a popular holiday resort with shops and supplies. Its main drawback is its popularity with wet bikes and small powercraft.

The headland of Porth Dinllaen approaching from Bardsey Sound

Porth Dinllaen. The red building is the Ty Coch pub (Ty Coch is Welsh for 'Red House')

Porth Dinllaen. Anchor clear of the moorings in 3m

PIPER'S EXPERIENCE BARDSEY SOUND

The wind was southerly force 4 as *Piper* beat along the Lleyn Peninsula from Porth Dinllaen: long tack offshore, short tack in. The ebb had been running for nearly two hours when at last Bardsey Sound opened to port. The wind, brisk in the lee of the peninsula, became uncomfortably fresh with open water to weather. In the entrance to the Sound there was a short, steep sea but *Piper* held her course and I was reassured by our good progress but as we came abeam of the Carreg Ddu the waves began to mount. *Piper* was now rising and plunging into the rearing seas and the spray came aft in bucket loads. Ahead the Devil's Ridge was visible as an area of broken white. I steered a course inshore of it, towards the relative calm of Aberdaron Bay, but it was impossible to avoid the confused water entirely and I was thankful that the jaws of Hell's Mouth were at least a couple of miles to leeward.

Despite the uncomfortable conditions *Piper's* speed over the ground was excellent and less than an hour after we had entered Bardsey Sound we were clear of the worst of it. Bringing *Piper* close hauled allowed us to clear the Causeway buoy on our southeasterly tack and we were soon making good speed towards Aberdovey.

If conditions had been too bad in Bardsey Sound we could have gone around the outside but this decision is best made early because once in the grip of the tide it can be difficult to break free. An offing of three or four miles would have avoided the worst of the overfalls but south of Bardsey Island is the Bastram Shoal which would then have stood between *Piper* and her objective, forcing us to beat further to the south. There would have been no avoiding the Devil's Tail, an area of overfalls stretching up to 10 miles south of Bardsey.

On the way home we had departed Aberdovey, thirty miles to the south, an hour or so before high water. It had been the plan to pass through Bardsey late on the flood with enough fair tide to see us up to Porth Dinllaen, eleven miles along the Lleyn, and then continue to Llanddwyn against the ebb, there to wait for the turn to carry us over Caernarfon Bar.

The light wind meant that we were cutting it fine to catch the last of the flood. As we approached the Sound we were only fifteen minutes late for slack water. *Piper's* ground speed slowed: on went the engine. *Piper's* ground speed continued to slow: the throttle opened wide. Eventually we stopped. I watched the shore as the engine tried to rattle itself free of its mountings. The shore remained stubbornly still, just short of the narrowest part of the sound. I edged *Piper* towards the Lleyn shore hoping to find a reverse flow. We went sideways but not forward. I edged *Piper* towards the Bardsey shore. We did a ferry glide along the invisible line on the water beyond which we could not move. I tried this for half an hour until *Piper* began to go backwards. Admitting defeat I turned *Piper* away from the Sound and made for the anchorage at Henllwyn Cove.

This is an exquisite spot and I spent a very relaxing afternoon enjoying the enforced indolence and listening to the seals as they snorted and splashed. At last, as the tide turned northwards once more *Piper* and I tried again at the Sound. This time we sped through effortlessly with the young flood and by nightfall had crossed Caernarfon Bar to anchor by moonlight in Abermenai Pool.

Contacts
South Caernarfon Yacht Club
VHF Ch 37
Fuel and chandlery Abersoch Land and
Sea Services
Chandlery Abersoch Boatyard
Marine Engineer Hookes Marine
☎ 01758 712458

Pwllheli

52°52´.7N 04°23´.3W
HW: Dover –0300
If conditions make the other anchorages
untenable, Pwllheli marina gives excellent
shelter and can be entered at all states of
tide and in almost all weathers. Pwllheli is
the largest town on the Lleyn. There are
all the services a yacht could need here
with shops, banks, etc. in the town.

Porth Dinllaen

52°57´.3 N 04°34´.1W
HW: Dover –0205
Porth Dinllaen is 11 miles from Bardsey
Sound. Anchorage can be had here with
good shelter in winds from east through
to west but in west to northwest winds
an uncomfortable swell sets into the bay.
There is good holding in mud, clear of
the moorings in 3m. During the summer
the Ty Coch (The Red House) pub is
open on the beach. The harbour was
once home to a small fleet of herring
fishing boats.

Facilities
Post office and small shops in Nefin.

CHARTS AND PILOTS

Imray C51, C52
Admiralty 1971
*Cruising Anglesey and Adjoining
    Waters* Ralph Morris (Imray)
Lundy and Irish Sea Pilot David Taylor
    (Imray)

**Smooth water in the
south of the sound
with no wind and the
ebb just beginning**

3. BRISTOL CHANNEL AND THE SEVERN

It's about a hundred miles from Milford Haven to Land's End across the mouth of the Bristol Channel; from Land's End to Avonmouth is 150 miles. This huge cleft in the coastline of Britain faces the prevailing westerly weather and is too far south for Ireland to offer protection from the open Atlantic. The coast of Wales, below its backdrop of hills and valleys, carries echoes of the coal and steel that once brought prosperity to the region. On the southern shore the green-topped cliffs of Devon and Cornwall stretch westwards, dotted with pretty fishing villages. The coastlines gradually squeeze together as you go east, compressing the tides. East of Hartland Point and Lundy Island tides strengthen considerably until at the Severn rates attain 8 knots where the river meets the sea at the Shoots, the stretch of turbulent, muddy water between the two bridges.

CROSSING THE MOUTH

Milford Haven is the ideal northern departure or arrival point for a passage across the mouth of the Bristol Channel.

Entrance is easy in any weather and at all states of the tide, although it can be rough in southerlies in what the locals call 'the washing machine'. The entrance is very well marked, the only caution being the very large ships that use the harbour. The crossing between Padstow and Milford Haven is about 65 miles and is one of the most exposed passages on the British coastline. If conditions deteriorate a yacht can find herself a long way from shelter. In westerly weather Lundy Island provides a useful refuge and staging post, being 32 miles from Milford and 37 from Padstow. The island is surrounded by tidal races and should only be approached near slack water. The most ferocious of these is the White Horses Race which forms over the Stanley Bank to the northeast of the island. Arrival at Padstow is best on a rising tide as the ebb runs hard in the river and if you want to lock in to the town quay you need to be there at HW±2. Otherwise, a mooring in the Pool may be available or anchorage in the River Camel estuary.

From Milford Haven to Land's End is about 100 miles. From the north it will be difficult to time your arrival for the turn of the tide at Land's End (Dover +0100). A good plan is to arrive with some time in hand to anchor off St Ives. The shelter is far from complete but from here it's easy to take the last of the ebb, picking up the young flood as you clear the Longships and head towards the Runnel Stone with a fair tide to carry you into Mounts Bay.

The Longships light at the tip of Cornwall, the western extreme of the Bristol Channel. From here to Avonmouth is over 150 miles

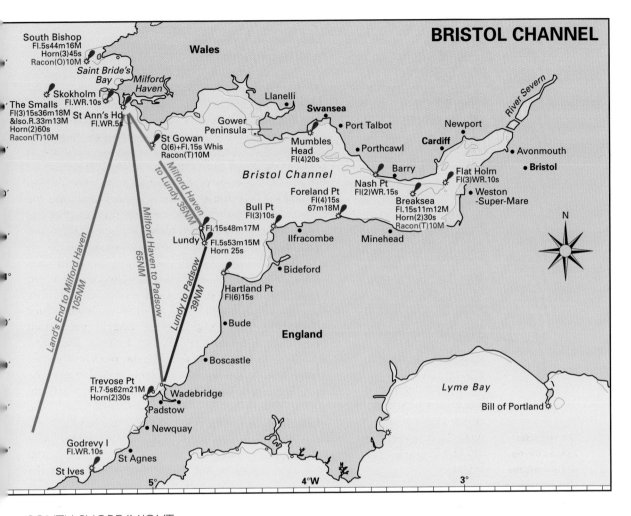

SOUTH SHORE IN/OUT

Making from Land's End towards Avonmouth, arrival off the Longships Light at low-water slack (Dover +0100) will avoid the worst of the overfalls there and give the assistance of a full flood in which to make Padstow. A skipper has the option of continuing against a foul tide from Padstow to Bull Point or of waiting out the tide in Padstow. The need to leave at low water means a berth in the Pool rather than locking in to the town quay. It would be a shame to miss out on this lovely Cornish harbour, but there are several anchorages that would serve if you want to avoid going up the Camel. Temporary anchorage may be found inside Stepper Point or if this is too exposed better shelter can be found in Porquin Bay.

'Get inside the Mouls and drop your hook close under the cliffs. You'll be as safe as houses in there.'

Trevor Platt, Padstow Harbourmaster

East of Bull Point the strength of the tide increases significantly and going against the flow will be a slow business. Good harbours are well spaced on this southern shore but Lundy and Ilfracombe are well placed for a stopover with Avonmouth within range on one tide.

PIPER'S EXPERIENCE CROSSING THE MOUTH OF THE BRISTOL CHANNEL

The wind was SW4 as *Piper* cleared the entrance to Milford Haven. Our intended landfall was Cape Cornwall, continuing around to Newlyn. The tide was just beginning to ebb and if all went to plan we would just catch a fair tide around Land's End in the early hours of the next morning. With *Piper* close hauled our heading was several miles to the east of Cape Cornwall but for now the tide was helping us up to windward and the forecast hinted at a freeing veer later in the day. I was full of high hopes as *Piper* bounded towards the southern horizon. An hour out and I took a back bearing on St Ann's Lighthouse, now fading astern. Clear of the land the sea was lumpy, with waves seeming to come from all directions at once and the wind against the tide. Below at the chart table I had the first hint that all would not go to plan. I rarely suffer seasickness but as I plotted my back-bearing on the chart my head started to swim and I dived for the hatch gasping for fresh air. Trusting it would pass, I held *Piper* on her course and for a

further three hours I stared at the horizon through gritted teeth. I felt cold and clammy and forays below were hasty visits to the chart table: two pencil lines and then back outside quickly. Eventually, I lost the battle and my breakfast and lay on the cockpit sole feeling utterly wretched. I calculated that I had another twenty hours to Newlyn. Time to think again. With the chart on a cockpit seat and a bucket at my elbow I plotted a course for Padstow. With luck I could be there in another eight or nine hours and would just make it in time to lock in to the inner harbour. The time passed miserably. I wrapped myself in as many warm layers as I could fit under my oilies and huddled in the cockpit, sipping water from a bottle and retching into the bucket. Every couple of minutes I raised my head above the dodgers to scan the horizon. *Piper* and the autohelm needed no assistance from me and we continued to make excellent progress. At last Trevose Head hove into view and soon *Piper* was nosing up the River Camel against the young ebb. We were cutting it very fine for the inner harbour lock but a call ahead meant that we were expected and the harbourmaster's cheerful wave welcomed us in and directed us to a berth. Within minutes

Piper was secured to a wall in perfect calm. Stepping ashore was an instant cure and I was suddenly ravenously hungry. A mountain of chips, a hot Cornish pasty and a pint of beer completed the therapy. I have crossed this stretch of water many times since, sometimes without any ill effects. At other times, even after many weeks at sea I take a precautionary Stugeron in case the confused wave patterns of the Bristol Channel have me reaching for the bucket.

PIPER'S EXPERIENCE BRISTOL CHANNEL INWARD AND OUTWARD

Inward

Homeward bound from France *Piper* was in Newlyn. It had been an easy, though windless, crossing and I hoped the forecast northwesterly would materialise in time to give us a good passage up towards Avonmouth where I had work to do. For now it was still flat calm. We motored out of Mounts Bay in the early afternoon, rounded the Runnel Stone and were off the Longships as the flood began, with a breeze too feeble to prevent the sails from slatting as we rolled in a heavy swell. Around Cape Cornwall the autohelm was working overtime as *Piper's* stern lifted to the seas that swept up under her quarter. It was slow, unpleasant work. By the turn of the tide, with no moon and still under engine, I was worried about running over a pot marker in the dark. Tired and frustrated, I turned *Piper* shorewards to drop anchor off Newquay, hoping to find some respite from the swell, behind the headland to the south of the bay. It proved to be a lively night but I took the sting out of the motion by hanging my sea anchor out on the boom end. Weighted with spare chain and hung down into the water, it

served to damp the roll to a considerable degree. Next morning was windless and foggy but as the forecast was for a clear day and I was unwilling to miss the fair tide I set out into the gloom on a track that would take me well offshore. The air had cleared by the time we were rounding Hartland Point and by evening *Piper* was at anchor in Ilfracombe.

There was a lot of ground to cover the next day. Lack of wind left it to the diesel to do the work and with *Piper's* speed under engine around 4½kn I entertained little hope of reaching Avonmouth before the tide turned. However, by Foreland Point our ground speed was already increasing. From Foreland Point I laid a course to pass north of Culver Sand and as Flat Holme became visible our ground speed had risen to 7kn. As I made my compulsory VTS report at EW Grounds our speed was almost 9kn. We locked in to the marina at Portishead with an hour to spare.

Outward

Piper had left Bristol City docks as early as possible and cleared Avonmouth to join the strengthening ebb in the King Road. The wind was light southwesterly and we made good progress aided by the strong tide. Flat Holme was bathed in warm evening light as we passed and by nightfall we were approaching Barry. Entry in the dark was fairly

straightforward and there was enough ambient light inside the outer harbour to find the mooring buoy, just astern of the lifeboat. Another yacht was already secured to the mooring and the skipper kindly invited me to raft *Piper* alongside. A quiet night and an early start found *Piper* sweeping westward on the next ebb, close hauled in the light SW wind. The water became more choppy as we neared Nash Point and *Piper* continued to accelerate in the strengthening tide. We crossed Swansea Bay in dying wind and approaching the Gower I started the engine, wanting to be clear into Carmarthen Bay before the tide turned. *Piper* was due south of Caldey Island by slack water. With the flood strengthening our ground speed steadily dropped. We crept around St Gowan's Head at a snail's pace and had ample time to admire the off-duty tanks parked along the cliffs at Castlemartin. Freshwater Bay opened eventually and as we passed into the entrance to Milford Haven the tide was on our side once more.

Piper at anchor in the outer harbour at Ilfracombe, well placed as a stopover when sailing in or outward in the Bristol Channel

NORTH SHORE IN/OUT

The north shore of the Bristol Channel has a greater choice of harbours and anchorages to break the trip or to wait out a foul tide. Shelter from most directions can be found at Caldey Island or nearby Tenby and a mooring in the outer harbour at Barry may be available for a short stay. Temporary anchorage can be found at several places along the coast but with big tidal ranges you need plenty of cable and swinging room. There are marinas at Swansea and Cardiff but if making a passage east or west the tidal restrictions on entering and leaving make it difficult to take advantage of a full fair tide. As with the south shore, tides are stronger the farther east you go, with a spring rate of 3kn off the Gower. To make a single passage between Milford Haven and Barry a strong fair tide east of the Gower more than compensates for the weaker adverse flow in Carmarthen Bay. From Barry eastwards it is a short passage to Avonmouth. A prompt departure brings within range the Avon to Bristol and the Severn, through the Shoots to Sharpness.

The Second Severn Crossing beyond the Cockburn PHM as *Piper* heads out into the King Road

THE SEVERN TO SHARPNESS AND BACK

The water of the Bristol Channel is progressively squeezed as it moves east with the flood tide. This compression produces the second biggest tidal range in the world, a staggering 12.2m mean spring range at Portishead compared with the 'modest' 6.3m at Milford Haven. The currents run strongly through the Shoots, up to 8kn in the narrows, often setting across the banks. This is a passage that requires care, but each critical leg is clearly marked by transit beacons so that with a little planning and a clear head it is possible to stay out of trouble.

Local yachtsman Colin Haigh says:

'If you stick to the timings rigidly and stay on the transits you'll be OK.
Outside these times it can be horrid.'

It is not advisable to go above the Severn Bridge before HW±0200, departing King Road not before HW Sharpness −0300. Leave the Cockburn PHM to port and make for the centre of the suspension span of the Second Severn Crossing, passing between the PH beacon (Fl(3)R.10s) on the Black Bedwins and the W cardinal beacon (Q(9)15s) on English Stones. Ahead on the Welsh shore the Redcliffe Beacon

gives a transit of 013°, with the white beacon on Charston Rock. Port and starboard marks are attached to the tower supports of the suspension span of the bridge.

Through the bridge a red beacon comes into view to port, the lower of a pair of transits. The rear transit mark is charted as being on the bridge astern, and leaving the Charston Rock to port would give a transit astern of 234°, a course of 054° between the Welsh shore and the Dun Sands. Hold this course towards the Welsh end of the Severn Bridge where a beacon (Fl.WRG) marks the extent of the rocks. Pass offshore of the bridge support tower but to the northeast of mid-channel. Beyond the bridge leave another beacon (Q.WR) to port and stay parallel with the shore until the transit lights come into view. These blue strip lights are hard to miss and give the next transit astern of 210°, a course of 030° inshore of Oldbury Sands to Inward Rocks through the Slime Road.

From Inward Rocks the channel changes sides, the leading marks giving a bearing astern of 252°, the course of

The unmissable blue light transits that see you safely through the Slime Road

072° passing north of the Counts N cardinal float. The Ledges SHM is just in front of a white bungalow on the shore. Between the white bungalow and a white house another pair of leading lights (2F) pick up the track on a transit of 070°. From the Counts these may be more easily picked out than the Inward Rocks astern. From Counts to the Ledges the channel passes to the north of the cooling water reservoir for the Oldbury Power Station. The next set of transit marks are pylon towers set within the reservoir. These give a transit astern of 224° for a course of 044° towards Hills Flats. Three sets of transits come rapidly in the next section, giving safe passage clear of the rocks at Hills Flats, Hayward Rock and Bull Rock which extend from the eastern shore. Past Hayward Rock the

Looking astern for the rear transit mark in the Shoots. (Is that a traffic camera on a pole or a nav mark on the bridge above the PHM?)

Chocolate milk shake? Turbulent, muddy water confused *Piper's* sounder and frightened her skipper

**The Inward
Rocks transit
marks**

Berkeley Power Station has a rectangular white board above the shore. On the end of one of the buildings a white square gives the transit with this to clear the Hayward Rock. As you approach the shore the Fishing House leading lights come into line off the starboard quarter. The front mark at the top of the bank is a white diagonal cross with orange-painted tips on a white conical pillar. Beyond this, partly hidden by the trees until you are nearly on the line, is a white rectangle on a pole. This transit astern of 217° takes you clear of Bull Rock on the reciprocal of 037°. The final transit is given by two white boarded lattice towers to the north of Berkeley Power Station.

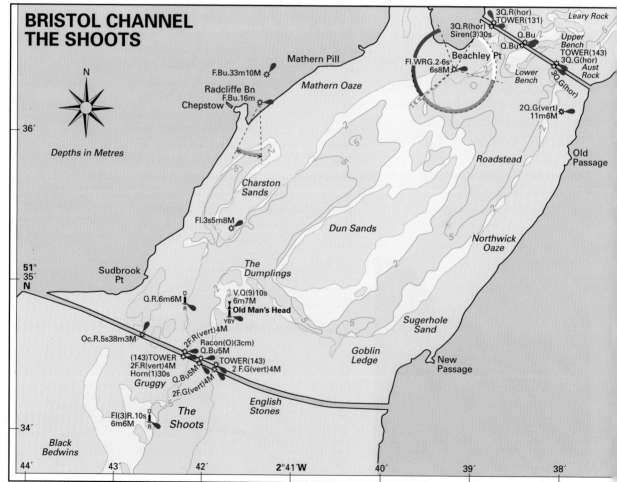

Bringing these in line astern on a bearing of 188° will carry you safely offshore of Sharpness dock entrance. The piers either side of the entrance look as if once between them you would be sheltered from the tide, which may be sluicing past the entrance at up to 5kn. On closer inspection, however, they are a wooden lattice construction and the water flows straight through them. Take care when entering that you are not swept alongside and pinned there by the force of the current. To starboard when inside is a holding pontoon where you can lie alongside until the lock opens.

Going downriver

The trip downriver is an exact reversal, leaving Sharpness just before local high water. If this is a return trip it is easier to identify the transits, having seen them on the way up, but there is no room for complacency. If all goes well you will have ample time to lock in to the comfort and tideless security of Portishead

The evening sun as we pass under the Second Severn Crossing on the way back to Portishead, relieved that we have passed up and down the lower Severn safely

Approaching the dock at Sharpness. The piers are pile construction and do not give the expected shelter from the run of the tide

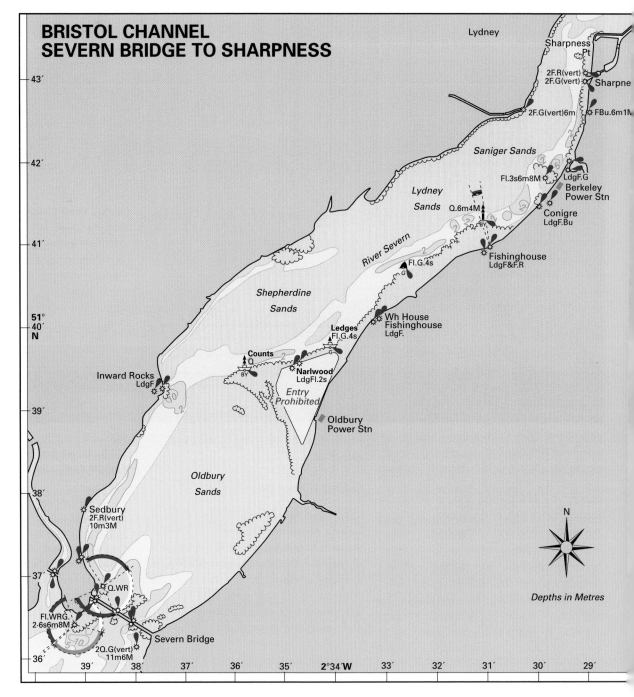

**BRISTOL CHANNEL
SEVERN BRIDGE TO SHARPNESS**

Lydney

Sharpness Pt

2F.R(vert)
2F.G(vert)
Sharpne

2F.G(vert)6m   FBu.6m1M

Saniger Sands

Fl.3s6m8M   LdgF.G

Lydney
Sands   Q.6m4M   Berkeley
Power Stn

Conigre
LdgF.Bu

River Severn

Fl.G.4s

G

Fishinghouse
LdgF&F.R

Shepherdine
Sands

Wh House
Fishinghouse
LdgF.

Ledges
Fl.G.4s

G

Counts
Q

Narlwood
LdgFl.2s

BY

Inward Rocks
LdgF

10

2

Entry
Prohibited

Oldbury
Power Stn

39′

Oldbury
Sands

N

38′

Sedbury
2F.R(vert)
10m3M

37′   Q.WR

Depths in Metres

Fl.WRG.
2·6s6m8M

Severn Bridge

2Q.G(vert)
11m6M

36′

43′   42′   41′   51°
40′
N

39′   38′   37′   36′   35′   2°34′W   33′   32′   31′   30′   29′

Marina. If you are making for Bristol City Docks then you will have a few hours to kill before it is possible to enter the River Avon. The commercial docks are off limits to pleasure craft but yachts have made temporary use of a floating stage inside the breakwater.

THE SEVERN BORE

The Severn Bore occurs on spring tides higher than 8m. The higher the tide, the more impressive the bore, a wall of water that roars upriver from Beachley to beyond Sharpness and on up almost to Gloucester. Fortunately for yachts passing upriver towards Sharpness the bore occurs early in the flood, well before a yacht would begin the passage.

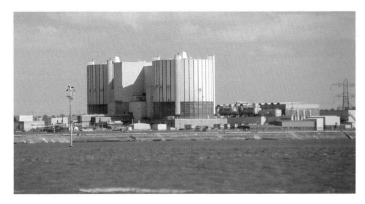

THE RIVER AVON

In the King Road the docks are prominent to starboard as Portishead Point is passed. At night the glare of the docks make identification of lights difficult. Identify the Cockburn PH buoy (Fl.R.5s). From here the south pierhead (Oc.RG.30s) is just south of west of here.

In daylight the square tower of Avonmouth Port Control is visible just beyond the light. As you enter the Avon inform Avonmouth Port Control that you are heading for Bristol City Docks, calling *Avonmouth Radio* on Ch 12. Leave the South Pierhead close to port, running parallel to the south pier until the Swash Channel leading marks are in line 127°, turning to 173° when the St George's leading lights, orange rectangles on white poles in front of the white-roofed buildings on the SW shore, are in line. Continue on this course until approaching the far shore then enter the narrows, keeping to the centre of the channel.

Oldbury Power Station from the Counts. The front leading mark sits in the station's cooling water reservoir

The 'white house' at Shepherdine is close to the foreward transits that lead across the Counts

The N cardinal marking Hayward Rock

The white transit beacons to the north of Berkeley Power Station give a clear course up to Sharpness dock

The transit marks in the Oldbury Power Station reservoir which give an astern transit to Hills Flats

Once in the river proper, navigation by day is straightforward. Keep generally to the middle of the channel but favour the outside of bends. Under the M5 motorway bridge keep to mid-channel. Pill appears to starboard half a mile farther on. With local knowledge it is possible to dry out here in soft mud. At the Horseshoe Bend the deepest water is on the outside of the bend. This is about half way. From here the land either side of the river gets higher until the Clifton Suspension Bridge. At night starboard-hand lights mark the channel. These are sometimes obscured by vegetation and are not very bright but do appear when needed.

At Black Rock lights are displayed, 1½ and 2½ cables above the suspension bridge. Fixed green means 'come ahead with caution', red means 'stop and await instructions'. If the red light is displayed on the docking signals mast at Hotwell's Pontoon contact the dock master on Ch

14. Failing this, proceed along the starboard side of the river outside the main channel. Secure alongside the knuckle ladder at Tongue Head and contact the dock master for instructions.

THE HARBOURS

Milford Haven

See 9. Jack Sound, Ramsey Sound & The Bishops.

Padstow

50°33′N 04°56′W

Padstow is on the north coast of Cornwall 50 miles from Land's End. Set within the shelter of the River Camel, it is the only harbour on this coast offering complete protection. Padstow was once the fourth most important harbour in the country, serving a thriving coastal trade and Cornwall's tin and china clay industries. The tiny harbour is right in the centre of the town and in the season gets

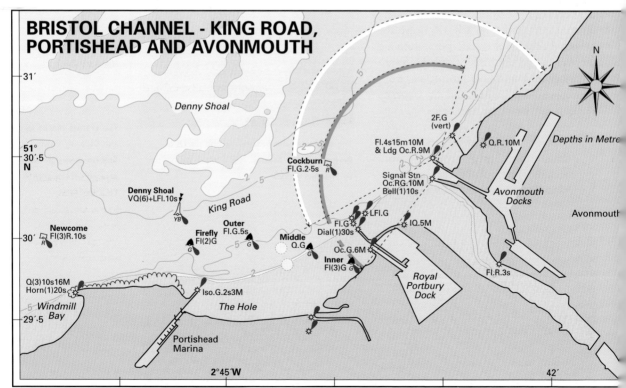

BRISTOL CHANNEL - KING ROAD, PORTISHEAD AND AVONMOUTH

very busy with visiting yachts, fishing boats and tripper boats. This is a very popular harbour, both because of its position and for what the town itself has to offer, so it's a good idea to call ahead to check the availability of berths. Trevor Platt will direct arriving yachts to a berth which will usually involve some rafting up and occasionally some tight manoeuvring. The yacht berths are normally to starboard as you enter. The lock gate, open HW±2hrs, maintains a least depth of 3m within the harbour.

Facilities

Much thought has gone into anticipating the needs of visiting yachts. There are showers, toilets and laundry facilities in the red-brick building on the north side of the harbour. Further showers and toilets and laundry are located in the harbour office on the south side of the entrance. Access is by keypad and the number code is given to you on arrival. Fresh water and electricity are available at all berths within the harbour. Electricity cards (£1 or £5) can be purchased from the harbour office.

The fuel berth is on the south pier but if you require diesel in cans just leave them outside the harbour office where they will be filled at 0900 and 1600hrs. Harbour staff will also do a petrol run to the local garage at those times. Calor and Camping Gaz can be purchased from the harbour office

Contact

Harbourmaster Trevor Platt

☎ 01841 532239 VHF Ch 16/12

Portishead Quays Marina

51°29´.7N 02°45´.1W

The marina is in the Portishead dock, 0.6 miles to the east of Portishead Point. The dock was first opened to relieve the problems of Bristol docks from larger shipping. The establishment of the marina in 2001 has greatly eased the logistics of navigating the Avon and upper Bristol Channel, offering 250 berths by spring 2004, rising to 400 berths when the project is completed. New lock gates maintain a least depth of around 5m within the marina. The outer cill is 3.0m above chart datum. Under normal conditions a yacht of 1.5m draft can access the lock HW±4.5hrs on mean neaps and HW±3.75 hrs on mean springs. Outbound locks run on the hour and half-hour, inbound locks run quarter to and quarter past the hour.

Facilities

Diesel on the pontoon to starboard just inside the lock.

Water and electricity on pontoons. Pre-

Two narrowboats approach Avonmouth from the Second Severn Crossing, having passed safely down through the Shoots from Sharpness

A yacht on a drying mooring in The Hole, just oputside Portishead Marina. This weird landscape of mountainous mud covers from half flood

Piper **in the lock at Portishead in company with inland sailors**

A large supermarket is opposite the leisure centre on Harbour Road, a 10-minute walk from the marina gate. There is a cash machine here too.

Portishead town centre with banks, post office and a range of shops is a further 5 minutes. A regular bus service runs from here to Bristol city centre.

Lock signals

RRR – Do not proceed, keep clear of lock gates.

GWG – Proceed on instruction from Marina Control.

Contact

☎ 01275 841941 VHF Ch 80
Portishead Quays Marina

Lundy

51°10′.0N 04°40′.0W

The Island is owned by the National Trust and is run as a bird sanctuary. The anchorage is in the bay to the north of Rat Island. The tidal range is up to 7 metres at springs, 3 metres at neaps.

In easterly winds shelter may be found at Jenny's Cove on the west of the island.

paid electricity cards available from marina office.

Laundry on ground floor of marina control building.

Weather forecasts are displayed daily on the marina notice board.

Chandlery and marine engineers on site.

PIPER'S EXPERIENCE PORTISHEAD TO SHARPNESS

Piper entered the lock at Portishead marina to lock out 3 hours before high water. With me on board was local yachtsman Colin Haigh as we sank into the depths of the lock. The sun vanished from sight beyond the greasy green walls rising on either side. Slowly the outer gates swung open to reveal a slit of brightly lit open water. Ahead a group of narrow boats making for the River Avon slid out into the open water. Colin cast off the lines and *Piper* followed. I had one eye on the sounder as we passed over the sill but I needn't have worried. Out into the King Road the tide was running hard and I brought *Piper* round onto a course for the suspension span of the Second Severn Crossing. Passing the Avonmouth docks Colin and I strained our eyes to make out the beacons marking the channel. A ship, the *Cork Sands*, passed ahead and under the bridge, neatly showing us the way, and I made out the red PH beacon off the Black Bedwins. It felt better to have a point of reference in the swirling water. Into the Shoots we were under the bridge in a flash and with Colin on the helm I had my eyes on the far shore to keep the Redcliffe Beacon in line with the

Charston Rock. As the Charston Rock loomed up I scanned astern trying to identify the rear transit to line up with the PH beacon. It was invisible to the naked eye, so I tried the binos. Colin had no better luck. The water swirled chocolate brown and the turbulence broke up the surface. The sounder was confused too, and with a dry mouth I put *Piper* on course for the support tower at the Chepstow end of the Severn Bridge. Passing under the elegant span of the Severn Bridge, I watched for the front transit mark that would take us up the Slime Road to Inward Rocks. Colin told me it was unmissable, and he was right. Even so, the bright blue light came as a surprise as it hove into view. Settled onto our new heading, things quietened down a little after the churning water of the Shoots. Now we settled into a rhythm, Colin pointing out the marks and points of interest from his seat at the helm while I scanned the chart so that my understanding could keep pace with our rapid progress. Across to the Counts the tide set us northward towards the Shepherdine Sands but then from the Ledges our course was again parallel with the flow. Past the Hayward Rock N cardinal beacon Colin watched for a rectangular white board above the shore, then a square painted on the end of a building, edged in black. We found them then watched

astern as the cross on the Fishing House front transit mark turned from edge to front on. Then the rear mark emerged from the trees. We swept onward. As we left the Berkeley Power Station astern the jetties at the entrance to Sharpness Dock came into view. In minutes we were abeam of the entrance. Colin swung *Piper* round to meet the flow and facing almost directly downriver we ferry glided in through the gap, continuing to ferry glide between the pile jetties until we finally found still water within the outer lock basin. The eighteen miles from Portishead had taken less then two and a half hours. We weren't staying at Sharpness so, much to the consternation of the lock-keeper, we swung round and headed back out to face the last of the flood in the Severn. Leaving with us were two narrowboats. With a pilot on board they were making the trip to Avonmouth to go up the Avon to Bristol. As we made our way back down the Severn the narrowboats took their own course, finding channels that would make *Piper*'s deep keel a liability. Together we passed through the Shoots and under the Second Severn Crossing in the late evening light. We exchanged a wave as they turned away for the Avon. The passage ended as it had begun, in the deep cleft of the Portishead lock.

PIPER'S EXPERIENCE RIVER AVON

Despite our good speed up from Ilfracombe we had arrived at Portishead on the last of the flood and were too late to continue up to Bristol. I was reluctant to lose a whole day for the sake of a couple of hours and, assured that it was possible, decided to go up the Avon on the next tide. This would mean an 0300 start from Portishead, negotiating the tortuous passage in the dark. There was no moon as *Piper* slid out of the lights of the lock into the blackness of the King Road. A call to Avonmouth Port Control had alerted them to my presence and I was reassured that there were no large shipping movements. Even so, I suffered a few anxious moments as my eyes adjusted to the dark and I struggled to get my bearings in this unfamiliar river. All the time the tide was rushing us on so I had to waste no time in getting my act together. At last I identified the red flashes of the Cockburn PH buoy from which I had laid off a bearing for the entrance to the Avon. Bringing *Piper*'s head round onto the bearing I could see the lights in the windows of the square control tower building. The occulting light on the end of the south pier head swept across in front of the tower as *Piper* was set upriver. I headed *Piper* up-tide until the light showed once more to the left of the tower, ferry gliding across the flow until I was out of the main strength of the tide. I called the Avonmouth Port Control.

'Yes we can see you below us now. Have a good trip to Bristol, sir.'

A silhouetted figure waved a hand from an upper window. I held to the wall until the transits across the Swash were in line, watching the soundings and searching the water for a green buoy in the light from the docks. Once past this buoy I was in the river proper and I began to leave the lights of the docks behind. At first the river was broad and the depth gave me no cause for alarm. Once past the motorway bridge the light grew less and the banks closed in. I called Bristol City Docks. The lock-keeper was expecting us, a comforting thought as I felt the way through the blackness that had settled around *Piper* like a blanket. The lights of the shore at Pill drifted by in ghostly silence and the air was laden with moisture. At each turn the dim green of a beacon ashore showed the way. At the Horseshoe Bend a white mist floated on the water and the beacon light shone as if through ground glass. My heart thudded: fog had not been included in my calculations. To port the fields sloped down to the water and I watched as wraiths of mist sank down the bank, hiding the river ahead. I held to mid-stream, feeling my way with the sounder. All the time my mind raced, trying to work out a plan for an orderly retreat. The fog lasted for only a quarter of a mile, then broke up into scattered rags. The banks rose darkly to either side until the stars were limited to a strip overhead. By contrast with the cliffs I could see that the sky was beginning to lighten as we rounded a bend to come in view of the Clifton Suspension Bridge. A call to the lock-keeper confirmed that the gate of the Cumberland Lock was open. Its lights obliterated all else until *Piper* slid into the grey interior. Hands reached out to catch lines. Voices of welcome from somewhere up in the dazzle echoed around the lock, and as the water rose the faces came into view.

St Ives

50°13´.4N 05°27´.9W

A very pretty little drying harbour, popular with artists and tourists. Access is limited to 2 hours either side of high water. Visitors' moorings are available for bilge keeled yachts. It is possible to berth alongside the west pier but not in the presence of a swell.

There are a few basic facilities, showers may be available at the yacht club and there is fresh water on the quay. The town has good shops.

Barry

51°23´.0N 03°15´.5W

Barry is a popular holiday resort. The commercial harbour is accessible to yachts at all states of the tide, though there is limited room in the outer harbour. A mooring is often available close to the lifeboat where yachts can await a fair tide, but yachts should not be left unattended.

USEFUL CONTACTS

Sharpness HM ☎ 01453 811862
Before making for Sharpness it is essential to warn the harbourmaster of your arrival.
Coastguard (Portishead)
☎ 01275 341128
Avonmouth Signal Station
Current conditions and shipping:
☎ 01179 822257
Portishead Quays Marina
☎ 01275 841941
Severn Area Rescue Association
☎ 01453 511003

CHARTS AND PILOTS

Imray C59, C58, C60, C7
Lundy and Irish Sea Pilot David Taylor (Imray)

Piper approaches the Severn Bridge in the Shoots

4. CAERNARFON BAR

The island of Anglesey (Ynys Mon) sits off the northwest corner of Wales. To sail around its rugged and varied coastline is to encounter almost every conceivable challenge known to the cruising sailor, from the rocks and reefs of the north and west coasts to the sandbanks and narrows of the Menai strait. Tides are strong throughout and, except in the Menai Strait, secure shelter is hard to find. It has been said, by one who has done both, that if you can sail around Anglesey then you can sail round the world.

Caernarfon Bar is at the southwestern entrance to the Menai Strait. It is an area of shifting sandbanks extending for three miles between Belan Narrows and the open water of Caernarfon Bay. The route through the sands moves with every storm, sometimes changing dramatically as the sea breaks through in one place or the gap closes in another. Bounded by the Lleyn Peninsula to the south and the west coast of Anglesey to the north, the Bar is open to the concentrated force of southwesterly winds. With the wind in this quarter the fetch is all the way from Wexford and, given the gradually shelving bottom in Caernarfon Bay, the seas that can build up on the Bar can be of terrifying ferocity.

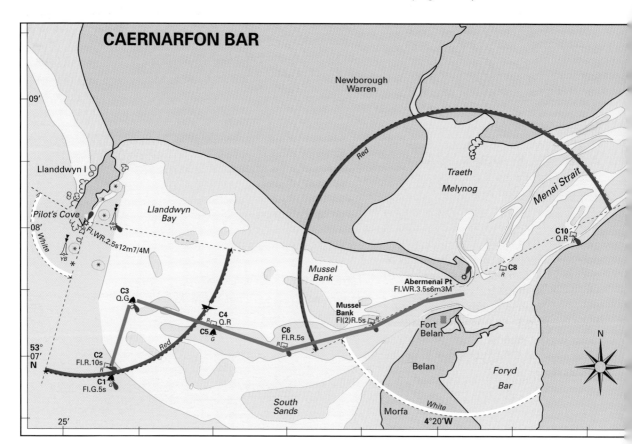

Approaching from seaward a yacht is faced with a distant line of sand dunes, before which stand the shifting sands of the Bar. From the Bar buoys C1 and C2 the entrance to the Menai Strait at Belan Narrows is hardly discernible. One clear mark is Llanddwyn Island at the northern end of the Bar. In strong W or SW winds the whole of Caernarfon Bay becomes a lee shore with a choice between hard rock to the north and sand to the south. If, after getting close enough to judge conditions at the Bar, a skipper decides to go elsewhere, he or she has a long way to go to find shelter.

At the inshore side of the Bar, Belan Narrows is the passage between Abermenai Point and Fort Belan. The Narrows are less than two cables wide and the tide through the gap exceeds five knots at springs. This is not usually a problem when inward bound as it speeds a yacht onward into the relative shelter of the Menai Strait. Outward bound, the Belan Narrows form a one-way gate. It is essential to be certain that conditions outside are suitable before committing to the Narrows. Without a lot of engine power, once through them there may no turning back for several hours. The nightmare is to pass through Belan with the door firmly slammed behind you, only to be met by breaking seas on the Bar.

CROSSING THE BAR

Inbound

The first visible mark when approaching from seaward are the white towers of Llanddwyn Island. The Bar buoys, C1 and C2, are approximately a mile south of the southernmost tower. They are surprisingly difficult to spot, even when you know where they are. One solution is to make a final approach on a course of 180° with Llanddwyn Island's light astern. This course will pass close offshore of the buoys. (This will be the normal approach anyway if it has been necessary to wait at Pilots' Cove.) Approaching from the west this is also a useful clearing bearing to prevent inadvertently venturing too close to the shallows.

Local practice is to cross the Bar after one hour of the flood. This has the advantage that the outer banks of the South Sands will not then be completely covered

C1 buoy is often hard to find when approaching from seaward. Three miles across the Bar, Belan Narrows are scarcely visible

It is best to cross the Bar as early as draft allows. David Taylor's *Lundy and Irish Sea Pilot* recommends entry no sooner than HW–0300. However, local practice is to cross the Bar after one hour of the flood. This has the advantage that the outer banks of the South Sands will not then be completely covered and will therefore afford some protection from the worst of any sea. Also, the breaking water on the banks will show their positions, making the channel easier to follow. This timing will also give a fair tide right up the Menai Strait, good timing for a safe passage of the Swellies and a little tide in hand to continue up to Beaumaris.

Before passing through the gateway of C1 and C2 it is wise to identify the starboard-hand buoy C3. The wreck of the *Grampian Castle* will be visible early in the tide, appearing well to starboard as you approach C3, though most of the wreck is now covered by sand or washed away. The channel runs to the south of the wreck, marked by port-hand buoy C4. In the region of C6 changes in the channel are frequent, sometimes requiring a sharp dog-leg, at other times the sea breaks through the sands and the dog-leg is removed. Do not assume that the next buoy you can see is the next one you head for. Changes to the buoyage are promulgated through local yacht clubs and harbour offices. Without recent

Approaching from the west a line of sand dunes is all that is visible beyond the Bar

information it is essential to contact Caernarfon HM to ascertain the latest positions of the buoys, or sometimes of the channel in relation to them. Alternatively, look at the Caernarfon Harbour website at www.caernarfonharbour.co.uk

In the outer reaches of the Bar the tides run fairly weakly, but approaching the Belan Narrows the strength gradually increases. Early in the flood the tides tend to follow the channel but, as the water level increases, the flow is across some legs of the route, particularly between C1/2 and C3; and C3 and C4/5. Avoid being set off course by watching that the buoy you are heading for is stationary against its background or by looking astern at the buoy you have just passed. Because of the speed of the tide past the Mussel Bank it is helpful to line up with the channel early, making sure Abermenai Point is open to the south of the Mussel Bank buoy soon after leaving C6 astern. The shores of the Narrows are steep-to, so if planning to anchor in Abermenai Pool begin to make the turn early in order not to be swept past, and stay within 50 metres of the Abermenai shore as you enter the pool on a northerly heading. There is an extensive drying bank between the point and the C8 red can, visible ahead as you emerge from the narrows.

Outbound

With moderate to strong westerly winds against an ebb tide the sea on the Bar can be very rough. Sheltered inside the Menai Strait there may be little to hint at conditions outside. Given that the best time to cross the Bar outward is in the first half of the ebb, the banks will be covered and the rough conditions may extend right inshore. Once through Belan Narrows it is too late for a change of heart unless you have a powerful engine and a good turn of speed. It would take about half an hour to drop the hook in Abermenai Pool and have a look at the sea from the top of the dunes. If the wind is west or southwest, Force 5 or over, or if you're just not sure, this could be time well spent.

Once out of the Narrows the Mussel Bank buoy comes up very quickly. It appears slightly to port as you emerge. Once it is identified, start looking for C6 as things move very fast in the strength of the tide. One regular chore for local sailors is to update the positions of the Bar buoys on charts and to update the waypoints for the crossing of the Bar on the GPS. These are set, not on the buoy positions, but in the channel near each buoy and saved as a route. Mark the waypoints on the chart including bearings (and reciprocals) and distances between each.

Local yachtsman Ian Rodger has many years experience of cruising the Irish Sea and farther afield. He agrees on the need for motor power if you want to fight the tide. He arrived just after high water on the wings of a SW6.

'There was no question of stopping. We ploughed on with fingers crossed. It was quite nasty and we got through Belan as the tide was rushing out. You definitely need a good engine.'

Ian Rodger

*'It can be an awful *!*! place, but treat it with respect and it's quite manageable.'*

Dave Galichan
Ex-cox'n Beaumaris Lifeboat

'We recommend high water plus or minus 3 hours, but temper that with the weather. Pilots survey the channel manually every year and notices are issued if there are any changes and posted in the Harbour Office and at Victoria Dock. Have a look at our website for up-to-date information.'

Capt. Gareth Jones
Caernarfon harbourmaster

C10 buoy is close inshore and must not be missed. Special buoy designs cope with the fast tides

PIPER'S EXPERIENCE CAERNARFON BAR

Fort Belan from the Narrows, with a yacht outward bound

Partly through luck and partly through a deep respect for its reputation, I have never been caught out by Caernarfon Bar. On the latest of many crossings I was returning from a visit to Cardigan Bay. Having missed the tide at Bardsey Sound I had spent the afternoon at anchor awaiting the turn and with evening advancing I raced along the Lleyn Peninsula. The sun sank into the sea astern as a full moon rose through rags of cloud above the mountains of Snowdonia. In the dusk I picked out the lights of the Bar buoys and made my approach. I used the hand bearing compass on the light of Llanddwyn for a clearing bearing to keep me out of trouble until I had read the

Belan Narrows in a fresh sou'westerly. The mountains of the Lleyn Peninsula form a backdrop

numbers on the buoys. The wind and sun had gone down together and we motored towards C3, its quick green flash near enough to see easily. C4 was harder to spot, its tiny red spark mixed in with the lights on the black outline of the shore and the pearly shimmer of moonlight spoiling my night vision. On the way out three days earlier I had checked my notes on the chart and updated my GPS waypoints. I brought *Piper* onto the required track and then looked ahead with the binoculars. I found the red flash

of the buoy and noted a group of lights on the shore behind it to act as a transit and to help me find it again among the other lights.

A similar strategy set me on course for C6 but its 5-second flash makes it harder to spot unless you happen to be looking right at it at the right moment. I strained through the binoculars, my mind probing the darkness. As I put the binos down a blacker triangle loomed up out of the darkness, outlined by the moonlight. I shoved the tiller hard over and held my breath as the unlit C5 buoy passed silently, very close to starboard. Past the Mussel Bank we swept into Belan Narrows. I headed *Piper* directly for the light on Abermenai Point and watched as the sounder came up to 5 metres. I followed this contour around the point, the dunes glowing dimly in the moonlight. In the Pool several yachts lay at anchor; none had an anchor light. I dropped my hook, set my own anchor light and turned in for the night.

IF YOU CAN'T CROSS THE BAR

Porth Dinllaen
52°57′.N 04°3′W
HW: Dover-0205

Approaching the Menai Strait from Bardsey with strong weather from south to west, alternative shelter can be found at Porth Dinllaen on the Lleyn Peninsula, 10 miles to the southwest. Fighting your way back to here from the Bar can be a long, weary business. An early decision to stop at Porth Dinllaen can save the hard beat out of Caernarfon Bay and is a good excuse to visit the pub on the beach. Anchorage can be had here with good shelter in winds from east through to west, but in west to northwest winds an uncomfortable swell sets into the bay. There is good holding in mud, clear of the moorings in 3m.

Llanddwyn Island
53°08′.0N 04°24′.7W
HW: Dover-0145

Except in winds from the south and east this is the perfect spot from which to time a crossing of the Bar. The rocky island at the northern end of Caernarfon Bar has two small bays on its eastern side, Pilots' Cove and Mermaid Cove. Pilots' Cove is easy to identify. At its southern arm is a white tower, lit at night (Fl.WR.2.5s12m7/4M). From seaward this is visible east of the disused lighthouse. Above the beach there is a row of small cottages, built to accommodate the pilots who used to operate from here. Shelter is excellent from the west through to northeast. In southwesterly weather the anchorage is subject to an uncomfortable swell but some protection from wind can be obtained by creeping as close inshore as possible into Pilots' Cove. The cliffs above the anchorage give an excellent view of the conditions on the Bar.

The abandoned lighthouse on Llanddwyn Island is a good mark from seaward. The pilots' cottages are visible to the right of the picture

Llanddwyn Island and
breaking water on the
South Sands around the
channel's seaward
entrance

Llanddwyn Island and breaking water on the South Sands around the channel's seaward entrance

Holyhead

59°19′.8N 04°37′.1W

HW: Dover-0040

Having arrived at the Bar at the beginning of the flood to find it impassable due to strong winds from south to southwest, Holyhead can be a useful alternative. Though it is almost 20 miles distant, the fair wind and over two knots of tide would make this a fast passage and possibly a pleasanter alternative to the beat down to Porth Dinllaen. However, this is a wild and rocky coastline. A good offing is advisable to avoid inshore dangers such as Carreg Goch off Rhosneigr and Maen Piscar off Treaddur. At South Stack, where the overfalls can be particularly rough, an offing of several miles may be needed given strong winds with a spring tide, but conditions improve rapidly once clear of North Stack and approaching Holyhead Bay.

Facilities here are good and it is possible to leave a yacht unattended in the marina. There are good rail links with the rest of the UK.

Caernarfon

53°09′.0N 04°16′.0W

HW: Dover –0130

Caernarfon is 2M NE from Belan Narrows on the mainland shore of the Menai Strait. Both the harbour and the Victoria Dock are accessible approximately HW±3hrs. 2m depth is maintained by a lifting cill in the Victoria dock. Entry is controlled by traffic signals. The harbour dries but it is possible to lean against the wall if space is available. Access to the harbour is through a swing (inwards) bridge. Request opening by one long blast on a foghorn when approaching. The bridge is left open at night. Once inside Victoria Dock or the harbour shelter is complete, but the tide sets very strongly across both entrances and in the channel, with steep breaking seas possible in strong winds.

Caernarfon is an interesting little town, dominated by its 13th-century castle, site of the investiture of Prince Charles as the Prince of Wales.

Abermenai Pool

53°08′.0N 4°20′.0W

HW: Dover-0115

A lovely spot and predictably popular, but well placed to time a crossing of the Bar outwards and keep an eye on conditions outside before committing to the Belan Narrows.

Approach the pool from due south keeping close inshore, about 20 to 50 metres off, but take care not to be drawn into the strength of the current pushing out through the narrows. If coming from Caernarfon direction resist the temptation to turn too soon. A drying sandbank extends to the west of C8. Holding is unpredictable due to the scouring effect of the strong tide through the pool.

USEFUL CONTACTS

Holyhead Coastguard ☎ 01407 762051
Caernarfon Harbour Master
☎ 01286 672118
Victoria Dock Gatehouse
☎ 01286 672346
Holyhead Marina ☎ 01407 762304

Marinecall (South of Colwyn Bay)
☎ 0891 500460
Check the latest info on
www.caernarfonharbour.co.uk

CHARTS AND PILOTS

Imray C52, C61
Admiralty 1464, 1970

Cruising Anglesey and Adjoining Waters
Ralph Morris (Imray)
Lundy and Irish Sea Pilot David Taylor
(Imray)

Caernarfon Castle and the harbour entrance from the Menai Strait

Oystercatchers on Abermenai Point at low water. On the horizon waves are breaking on the outer limits of the Bar

5. CARMEL HEAD AND THE SKERRIES

In the nineteenth century Carmel Head was an important landfall for sailing ships making for Liverpool, having sailed up the Irish Sea bringing goods from the farthest parts of the world. Shipowners in the port could be informed of their ship's arrival off the headland by way of a semaphore system. Ships' names were passed by way of Mynydd Eilian, Puffin Island, Great Orme and Hilbre Island off the Wirral in as little as five minutes. But though the ships' owners and crews would be relieved at the vessels being so close to the end of their voyage, they would not want to pass too close to Carmel Head.

This northwestern tip of the Isle of Anglesey is guarded by dangerous rocks and reefs. The Skerries is a group of rock islets half a mile long which stands 2 miles offshore. Today it is marked by a lighthouse. The original light on this rocky island was a fire, kept burning at night by a man and his wife who lived out there for that purpose. Inshore from the Skerries lie West Mouse and an assortment of smaller but no less lethal hazards. Three miles east of Carmel Head and standing right in the way of both yachts and tide is the reef variously named Harry Furlong , Harry Furlong's Rocks and Harry's Furlong, a jagged line of rocks just awash at low water which extends from the western arm of Cemlyn Bay. I like to imagine its name derives from 'Old Harry's Furlong', leaving no doubt as to who gets the blame for its devilish presence across the track of passing craft.

The north coast of Anglesey is set about with offshore rocks throughout its length. In good visibility these are not a

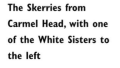

The Skerries from Carmel Head, with one of the White Sisters to the left

CARMEL HEAD AND THE SKERRIES

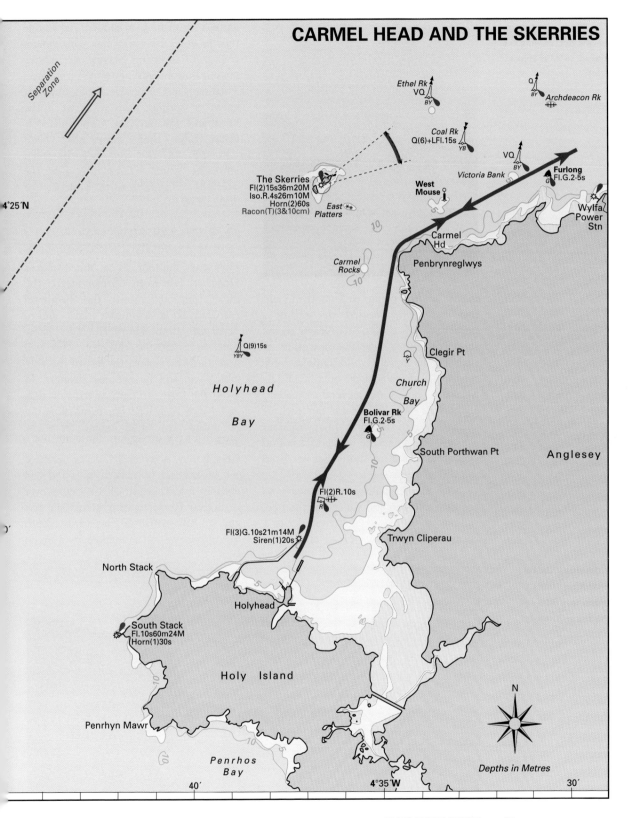

Separation Zone

Ethel Rk
VQ
BY

Q
BY
Archdeacon Rk

Coal Rk
Q(6)+LFl.15s
YB

VQ
BY

Victoria Bank

Furlong
Fl.G.2·5s
G

The Skerries
Fl(2)15s36m20M
Iso.R.4s26m10M
Horn(2)60s
Racon(T)(3&10cm)

East
Platters

**West
Mouse**

Wylfa
Power
Stn

Carmel
Hd

Penbrynreglwys

Carmel
Rocks

4°25′N

Q(9)15s
YBY

Holyhead

Bay

Y

Clegir Pt

*Church
Bay*

Bolivar Rk
Fl.G.2·5s
G

South Porthwan Pt

Anglesey

Fl(2)R.10s
R

Fl(3)G.10s21m14M
Siren(1)20s

Trwyn Cliperau

North Stack

Holyhead

South Stack
Fl.10s60m24M
Horn(1)30s

Holy   Island

N

Penrhyn Mawr

Depths in Metres

*Penrhos
Bay*

40′

4°35′W

30′

The White Sisters from up the hill, showing the transit to West Mouse

around it, making a sudden right-angle turn to enter Liverpool Bay. This violent change of direction occurs over a very uneven bottom, adding to the turbulence. Tidal rates at Carmel Head can attain 6.1 knots at springs midway between the head and the Skerries. Closer inshore, faster rates than these have been reported. In the presence of even moderate winds against this tide the overfalls can achieve a violence of destructive force.

AN EASTWARD PASSAGE

Holyhead harbour is 5 miles across Holyhead Bay from Carmel Head. The ideal time to round the headland eastward is at low-water slack and a departure from Holyhead must allow time to cover the distance. This will necessarily be against the last of the ebb, which will still be running strongly. To avoid the main strength of the tide tuck as far into Holyhead Bay as possible but be aware that rocks extend from the shore between Trwyn Cliperau and Church Bay. A wreck 0.7 miles north of the breakwater is marked by a red can and has a least depth of 8.5 metres over it. Bolivar Rock, halfway across the bay and 0.8 miles offshore, has a least depth of 2.2 metres and is marked by a green

major hazard, being well marked, and may be easily avoided by staying a prudent distance offshore. Nearer to the shore there are overfalls downtide of each of the hazards and unpredictable tidal sets, especially in the area of Middle Mouse. There are several excellent anchorages along this coast but each of them is open to the north. In any weather from that direction the whole rock-bound coast becomes a lee shore that has been the end of many ships.

This area would require care to navigate safely in still water but the tide, running up the Irish Sea at around 2 to 3 knots, reaches Carmel Head and pivots

Approaching Carmel Head West Mouse comes into view and the sea gets rougher

buoy. The shore is steep-to and clean from Clegir Point at the north side of Church Bay to Carmel Head.

Around Carmel Head there is ample depth right up to the foot of the cliffs. When the tide is running the smoothest water is to be found close in. From Trwyn Cerig-yr-eryr stay within a cable of the shore, looking ahead to spot the smoothest water. Hold this distance off until the transit beacons on the north side of the headland come into line. This will take you inside the Passage Rock. If overfalls are encountered it is at this point between Passage Rock and Carmel Head that they are at their most severe.

Once past the transit beacons the next hazard is the Victoria Bank. This is marked by a N cardinal buoy but the inshore route passes inside to the south of it. Having rounded the corner, typically just after low water, the tide will now be gathering speed, causing considerable turbulence over and around the Victoria Bank which has a least depth of 1.8 metres. A course of 064° from close under Carmel Head will take you clear but runs perilously close to Harry's Furlong. Speed over the ground will now be quite surprising so a good watch ahead must be kept for the Furlong starboard-hand buoy, which may well come up sooner than you expect and must be passed on its offshore side. I once averaged 10kn over the ground between Carmel Head and Point Lynas.

Once clear of the Furlong buoy things calm down and in settled weather from southerly quarters the anchorages of the north coast are a fascinating, if challenging, cruising ground. If conditions allow a visit to this coast a passage round Carmel Head from the west may be made on the last of the flood, allowing time to tuck into one of the anchorages before the tide turns hard against you. But be warned, if the weather comes in from the north you will have to clear out promptly.

South Stack

Northerly winds around this headland create very rough conditions, extending for several miles offshore on the flood. The rocky shore will be to leeward and considerable fetch to windward. In such a situation you have to be sure it's worth going around the north of Anglesey at all. Making for the Menai Strait, or even Conwy, the benefits of the shorter passage are questionable in such conditions. A safer plan would be to avoid Carmel Head altogether and wait for the ebb in the safety of Holyhead, reaching the Menai Strait via Caernarfon Bar, bad enough in its own way but rarely a problem in northerlies.

Overfalls extending out from South Stack. At such times an offing of 2 miles is advisable

Steep and confused seas off Carmel Head with many curling and breaking. Speed over the ground is 8kn. With the 10kn westerly wind reduced to 2kn over the deck, *Piper* needed the motor to maintain adequate steerage way

A WESTWARD PASSAGE

Timing is crucial in making a westbound passage and the direction of the prevailing wind makes wind against tide more likely on the ebb than the flood. From the shelter of the Menai Strait to Carmel Head is over 20 miles and working out the time this passage will take is a difficult calculation. Arriving

early at Carmel Head will result in a shaking; arriving late will mean being turned back by the tide. A safe plan is to leave in good time to avoid being late and, if when you arrive off Cemaes Bay you are too early tuck into the bay, to wait. Cemaes is a broad bay, easy of access and unmistakable due to the presence of Wylfa nuclear power station on its west side. Alternatively, use Cemlyn

Point Lynas, its lighthouse gazing out across the Irish Sea

Bay to the west of the power station and a mile closer to Carmel Head, but beware Harry's Furlong when you depart as the ebb will still be running and setting hard across the mouth of the bay onto the rocks.

From Harry's Furlong you should be able to judge the state of the sea off the headland. There will be little you can do about it now if you don't like what you see but this is a good time to check that the foredeck hatch is tightly closed. With the tide running, broken water extends out towards West Mouse but close under the cliff there is usually a gap, often only 50 metres wide but there is deep water right up to the foot of the cliff. From Passage Rock the pain will be short-lived as your speed over the ground will probably be in excess of 10kn and in less than a mile you will be round the corner. The overfalls extend southwest over Carmel Rocks so by staying close inshore as you enter Holyhead Bay you will soon find smoother water.

ALTERNATIVES TO THE INSHORE ROUTE

In conditions of fresh to strong winds from a northerly quarter or against the tide the inshore passage is not to be recommended as steep, damaging seas can develop when the tide is running. Slack water is of very short duration and the consequences of getting it wrong will be at least unpleasant, if not dangerous. Added to this is the local effect of the

Skerries lighthouse

Wylfa nuclear power station

Trwyn Du lighthouse

headland on the wind, creating turbulence and strong gusts on the downwind side.

To pass outside the Skerries in moderate weather a good offing is needed to avoid the roughest areas. Making eastwards from Holyhead pass south of the Langdon Ridge and follow the inshore edge of the Skerries TSS. Hold this distance offshore until north of Point Lynas. The route for a westward passage outside the Skerries follows a similar course but you will need to take care to stay out of the TSS as you will now be going contrary to the direction of the inshore lane.

The mountains of Snowdonia form a magnificent backdrop to the Menai Strait

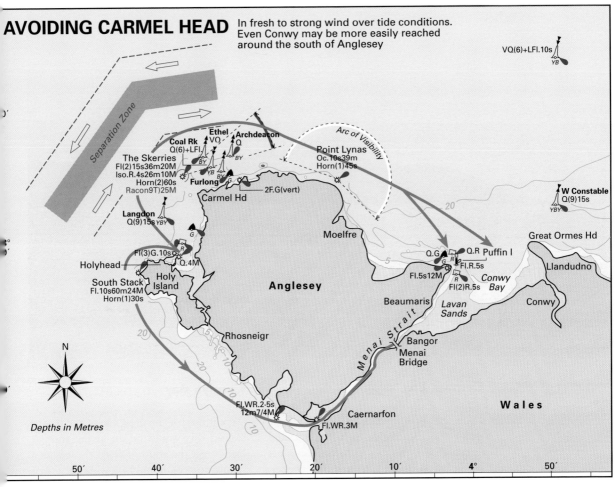

AVOIDING CARMEL HEAD

In fresh to strong wind over tide conditions. Even Conwy may be more easily reached around the south of Anglesey

VQ(6)+LFl.10s
YB

Separation Zone

Ethel VQ **Archdeacon** Q
Coal Rk Q(6)+LFl.
BY
The Skerries BY
Fl(2)15s36m20M
Iso.R.4s26m10M
Horn(2)60s **Furlong** G
Racon9T)25M
Carmel Hd
2F.G(vert)
YBY

Arc of Visibility

Point Lynas
Oc.10s39m
Horn(1)45s

W Constable
Q(9)15s
YBY

Langdon
Q(9)15s YBY
G
R
20

Moelfre

Great Ormes Hd

Fl(3)G.10s
Holyhead Q.4M
**Holy
Island**
South Stack
Fl.10s60m24M
Horn(1)30s

Q.G R Q.R **Puffin I**
G R Fl.R.5s
Fl.5s12M
R
Fl(2)R.5s

**Conwy
Bay**

Llandudno

Conwy

Anglesey

Beaumaris **Lavan
Sands**

N

Rhosneigr

20
15
10
20

Menai Strait

Bangor
**Menai
Bridge**

Wales

Depths in Metres

Fl.WR.2·5s
12m7/4M
Fl.WR.3M

Caernarfon

10

50´   40´   30´   20´   10´   4°   50´

A route is marked on Admiralty chart 1977 which passes midway between Carmel Head and the Skerries then between the Victoria Bank and Coal Rock. Whilst interesting in good conditions and with greater searoom than the inshore route, the transit of North and South Stack passes perilously close to the East Platters which dries 1.5metres at LAT and so will be just awash at most low waters. This course also passes through the areas of overfalls north and west of Carmel Head for a distance of about 5 miles, prolonging the agony.

ANCHORAGES

The Skerries Lagoon

Despite its position in the midst of such turbulent waters, there is an anchorage at the Skerries which is sheltered from the powerful tides. However, the anchorage is subject to sea and swell and should only be used in settled conditions. Approach from the southwest with Gull Rock, the most northwesterly of the group, on a bearing of 055°. This will take you inside African Rock. Though narrow, West Gully has 5 metres. Enter on a roughly easterly course, about 25 metres to the south of Trench Rock. There is a strong tidal set across the entrance.

Rough water off Point Lynas

Cemaes Bay

There are several choices of anchorage within this wide bay, depending on wind direction. In westerlies the small cove just inside Lamb Island gives the best shelter, the nuclear power station adding its bulk to keep the wind out. In easterlies Llanbadrig bay gives excellent shelter and by creeping close in some protection can be had from northeasterlies but a scend will make life very uncomfortable.

Cemaes village is set in the southeast corner of the bay and there is a small drying harbour. There is a shop in the village and an infrequent bus service to Holyhead.

Cemlyn Bay

Were it not for the presence of the power station this would be an idyllic spot. A lagoon on the south side of the bay is a nature reserve, home to a wide variety of wading and seabirds, and makes access from landward difficult. Whilst shelter is good from southeast through to southwest it is not the place to be in winds north of this.

HARBOUR INFORMATION

Holyhead

Holyhead is the largest harbour in the area. It is accessible in all weathers and at all states of the tide, making it a good refuge in rough weather. The ferry to Ireland operates from the ro-ro terminal and a good watch must be kept for high speed ferry movements.

The marina is on the west side of the harbour, overlooked by Holyhead Sailing

Club. There is water and power alongside, showers and toilets. There is a boatyard and chandlery and there is a sailmaker nearby. Diesel is available in the fish dock. The town is a short walk from the harbour and has a range of shops. Inter-city services run from the railway station.

Contact
Harbourmaster ☎ 01407 762304
VHF Ch 16, 14

Amlwch

This is the only harbour of any sort on the north coast. The entrance is protected by a wall built to service a now disused oil pipeline terminal, but the approach is exposed to swell and tide, making entry difficult in rough weather. If caught out on the north coast this can be a more appealing option than seeking shelter to the east - a passage of at least twenty miles - or of trying to round the northwest corner of Anglesey to Holyhead. The outer harbour is subject to surging swell in strong northerlies and

better protection is available in the pens in the inner harbour. These are much used by local fishing boats and permission must be obtained before berthing here.

There are a tap and public toilets on the jetty. In the village there are shops for provisions and a bus service to Holyhead.

The breakwater light, Holyhead

Amlwch: the entrance to the concrete breakwater

PIPER'S EXPERIENCE CARMEL HEAD & THE SKERRIES

Westward

I had anchored overnight at Moelfre and waited through a drizzly morning for the turn of the tide, impatient to be away. The tide turned and I continued killing time, cramped below and too damp to be on deck. At last I could stand the indolence no longer and pulled up the anchor with three hours to go before slack water at Carmel Head. I had fourteen miles to the headland and with the light wind reckoned I would time it about right.

Sailing towards Lynas *Piper* was making less than three knots through the water but on reaching Lynas we were already ahead of time and the damp zephyr had settled southwesterly. We were on spring tides and the water was troubled off Lynas despite the light breeze. *Piper* continued to make around three knots through the water but our speed over the ground increased markedly once north and west of Lynas.

I kept *Piper* close inshore, admiring the rugged coastline from fairly close quarters. The old brickworks in Porth Wen showed briefly, then as we passed inshore of Middle Mouse the tide set us towards the island. I steered a little towards the Anglesey shore. Still we seemed to be on a collision course with the rock. I headed *Piper* further inshore but the sails emptied and the genoa backed. I quickly tacked the sail and headed directly inshore. I could now see directly the speed of the tide as the north shore of Anglesey slipped across *Piper*'s bow. I held this course until I was sure we would run clear of Middle Mouse and then returned to our

original westward heading.

No sooner had I done so than she sailed straight into a hole in the sea. Downtide of Middle Mouse there was a visible depression in the sea surface. *Piper* dropped into it with alarming suddenness and popped out at the other side with a lurch. She continued her headlong rush and the light wind was now creeping up from ahead, partly as a result of *Piper*'s speed over the ground. I rolled up the headsail and started the engine, anxious to maintain sufficient steerage way to react quickly to the eddies.

I was already looking ahead for the overfalls off the headland, and though aware that we were early I pressed on. The grey wall of the nuclear power station loomed up and I thought it might be a good idea to pull in. I was still considering this option as we passed off Cemlyn Bay. The tide made the decision for me and I scanned inshore for the Furlong buoy, then as I looked ahead I spotted the green cone off to starboard of the forestay. We were too close in. I heaved the helm over and *Piper* swung out away from Anglesey. When I could see clear to Carmel Head outside of the buoy I returned *Piper* to her course. We had been a good bit away from Harry's Furlong but the speed over the ground was impressive so there had not been a huge margin for error.

Ahead now I could see the white water off the headland, a standing wave about a metre and a half high and curling at its crest. I squinted at the afternoon light for the smoother inshore gap. The white extended from the cliff foot to West Mouse without a break. *Piper* rushed at the wall and started to climb over it but, as is her habit, her stem cut straight in some way below the crest. As she rose

the wall of green water poured aft, dividing around the mast, sluicing onto the side decks and back over the coachroof. I watched in fascination as the deluge seemed to rear up in slow motion before hitting me full in the face. The world returned to normal speed and *Piper* dropped down the other side of the wave, rising and falling as if running down a river. We only took the one wave aboard and not much of it landed in the cockpit (I think it went down my neck instead). Soon we were round the corner and the fair tide across Holyhead Bay had us alongside the pontoon in a little over half an hour. Within an hour of my soaking I had rubbed a towel over my head, changed into dry clothes and walked up to Holyhead Yacht Club to order a beer and an excellent meal.

Eastward

Piper lay to a mooring in Holyhead and few clouds marred the tourquoise sky in the golden early light. The wind had been fresh northwesterly overnight and I had reservations about using the inshore passage. At 0630 I dropped the mooring, sailing off it in blissful silence under a main with a precautionary reef tucked in. It's sometimes hard to tell what's happening the other side of Holyhead's huge breakwater and I'd always rather shake a reef out at leisure than pull one down under pressure. As so often happens in Anglesey's strong tidal waters, I was not alone as I began the passage. Two other yachts were going the same way and the tidal gates demand that we all leave together. This is reassuring at times but if you are the only boat moving you tend to wonder, 'What's wrong? Have I missed something?'

To lay a course for Carmel Head *Piper* was pinching up to windward so I sheeted the reefed main flat and motorsailed. The wind was light, 10kn at most, and I knew I would soon need that extra power. The seas increased as we neared the headland and I had advance warning as the Sadler 32 ahead began to throw spray into the air. *Piper's* low freeboard meant that her decks were already wet but she rode comfortably, making good speed. Close to the headland the seas steepened and the strength of the tide gave us 8kn over the ground for a log speed of 4kn. The wind over the deck was now reduced to around 2kn and *Piper* needed the motor to maintain adequate steerage way in the steep and confused seas.

The Sadler now headed offshore to pass outside West Mouse. The other yacht had already taken a more offshore line, passing outside Carmel Rocks, and was midway between the Skerries and West Mouse. *Piper* was closest to the shore, holding a track about 100 metres from the cliff. This gave her the shortest track and an extra push from the tide yet in smoother water than is found further out. I watched as the two white beacons on Carmel Head appeared and gradually came into line then laid a course to clear the Furlong buoy which I could make out against the silver glare off the sea.

Piper was no longer kicking up spray and with the change in angle I was able to unroll the genoa and make use of the wind; though with the strengthening tide it added little to our speed, it served to steady the motion. Off the Victoria Bank the seas were very confused, spray leaping into the air, but the waves were not big and *Piper* passed unheeding. The mass of the power station loomed up and we passed safely off the Furlong buoy, breathing a quiet sigh as the waters ahead opened up.

I headed *Piper* for the gap inshore of Middle Mouse. In stronger winds I would want more distance between us and the rocky shore but the tide squirts through the space and would give us a good lift on our way. As we passed the island birds wheeled in the air above their crowded colony. Suddenly the stench of guano hit my nostrils and the romance of the previous moment was quenched.

The little bays of the north coast passed in turn and the concrete breakwater of Amlwch opened, picked out clearly in the slanting light. Ahead Lynas stood gazing out northwards. The overfalls here kicked up a little chop but the wind was dying and there was no malice in it. I rounded the light and the low outline of Puffin came into view, black against the silver and blue of the sea and sky. The motor had been running all the way along the north coast, insurance among the rocks in the strong tides and light winds. I pulled the stop button, silenced the alarm and let the autopilot do the work as we ghosted towards the Menai Strait and home.

**A quiet evening on a
mooring in Holyhead**

6. CHENAL DU FOUR

Sailing westwards down-Channel the French coast stands to port until you reach Ouessant, the 'Island of the West'. This northwest corner of France is a turning point for ships coming in from the Atlantic from all corners of the world, guided by the Pointe de Creac'h lighthouse with a range of 30 miles at the top of its 70 metre high tower. For a yacht from the south coast of England, having sailed westwards from some days, this corner of France is the gateway to lower, warmer latitudes. It is also a turning point for tides and currents sweeping in from the open ocean and faces full into the unfettered fury of sea and weather. Passing outside of Ile d'Ouessant can be very rough. The Chenal du Four rounds this corner within the shelter of the offshore islands. However, it has a reputation for unpleasantness of its own and demands considerable respect from the yachts that pass this way.

This is a treacherous coastline. Rocks and shoals extend some distance from the shore and the tides run very hard. Harbour entrances are set about by hazards. Fortunately, dangers are well charted and clearly marked and, being solid rock, do not generally move under the effects of tide and storms. By the same token, a grounding will certainly result in serious damage so the area demands careful and accurate navigation and a constant awareness of the set of the tide and its effect on your track.

FROM L'ABERWRAC'H

The tide turns about half an hour earlier in the Chenal du Four than at L'AberWrac'h, so a departure as the ebb begins there will deliver you to the Four when the tide there is almost at its full strength. Winds from the northwest will kick up a bad sea off the northern entrance to the Chenal du Four until you gain the shelter of Ile d'Ouessant, especially against a west-going tide, but even in the presence of an east-going tide the seas can be unpleasant. With winds from the south the Chenal itself can be bad, especially in the area from Le Conquet to Pointe de St Mathieu.

Leaving L'AberWrac'h an hour or so before high water take the Grand Chenal, passing the Libenter buoy

Le Conquet from the Grand Vinotière port-hand beacon

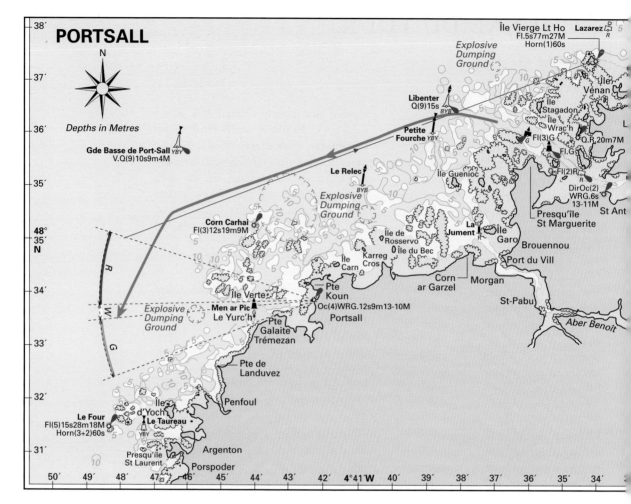

(Q(9)15s 8m6M Whis) to starboard. The reefs of Basse Trouquenou lie close to port. Do not turn from the Grand Chenal transit (100°) until the Petite Fourche W cardinal spar buoy bears 180°. From here a course of 250°, to pass north of the Basse Paupian W cardinal buoy, will clear all the hazards along this coast which extend up to 2½ miles offshore.

There are irregular tidal sets across this track so a back bearing of 070° on the Ile Vierge Lighthouse (Fl.5s77m27M Horn 60s) will be useful to keep you out of danger. From Basse Paupian a course of 205° will pass half a mile off the Four lighthouse (Fl(5)15s27m18M Horn(3+2)60s) from where it is 5M on a bearing of 190° to a point midway

between La Valbelle (Fl(2)R.6s Whis) and Les Plâtresses (Fl.RG.4s17m6M).

South of La Valbelle the tide is compressed by the rocks and islands to the west which slant inwards from Ile d'Ouessant, 10 miles west of the Four, to Ile de Beniguet, only 2 miles from Pointe de Kermorven. The flow accelerates as you go south. Between St Pierre and St Paul, the maximum spring rate is 2.3kn, increasing off Pointe Kermorven to a maximum spring rate of 5.0kn. Off Pointe St Mathieu the maximum spring rate is 3.2kn.

From La Valbelle, Pte St Mathieu and Pte Kermorven lighthouses are in line bearing 015°30´. If these are not visible it is possible to buoy-hop to St Paul

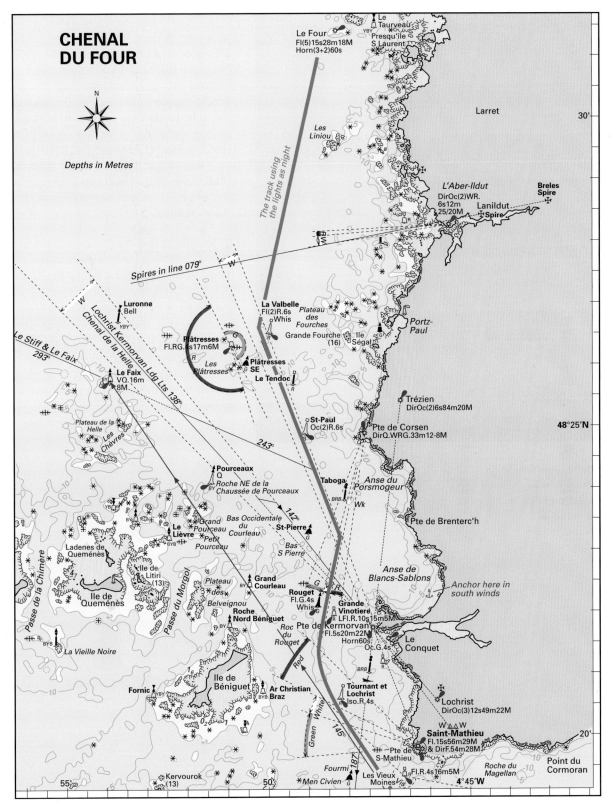

CHENAL
DU FOUR

N

Depths in Metres

Le Four
Fl(5)15s28m18M
Horn(3+2)60s

Le
Taurveau
Presqu'île
S Laurent

Larret

*Les
Liniou*

*The track using
the lights as night*

L'Aber-Ildut
DirOc(2)WR.
6s12m
25/20M

Lanildut
Spire

Breles
Spire

Spires in line 079°   W

Luronne
Bell
YBY

La Valbelle
Fl(2)R.6s
Whis

*Plateau
des
Fourches*

Grande Fourche
(16)

Ile
Ségal

Portz-
Paul

Lochrist Kermorvan Ldg Lts 138°
Chenal de la Helle

Plâtresses
Fl.RG.4s17m6M

*Les
Plâtresses*

**Plâtresses
SE**
Le Tendoc

Le Stiff & Le Faix
293°

Le Faix
VQ.16m
8M
BY

*Plateau de la
Helle*

*Les
Chèvres*

243°

St-Paul
Oc(2)R.6s

Trézien
DirOc(2)6s84m20M

Pte de Corsen
DirQ.WRG.33m12-8M

48°25'N

Pourceaux
Q
*Roche NE de la
Chaussée de Pourceaux*
BY

*Anse du
Porsmogeur*

Taboga
BRB

Wk

Pte de Brenterc'h

*Grand
Pourceau*
**Le
Lièvre**
BYB
*Petit
Pourceau*

142°

St-Pierre
G

*Bas Occidentale
du
Courleau*

*Bas
S Pierre*

*Anse de
Blancs-Sablons*

*Anchor here in
south winds*

*Ladenes de
Quéménés*

*Ile de
Litiri
(13)*

*Plateau
des
Belveignou*

**Grand
Courleau**
BY

Rouget
Fl.G.4s
Whis

G   R

**Grande
Vinotière**
LFl.R.10s15m5M

*Ile de
Quéménés*

Passe de la Chimère

Passe du Morgol

**Roche
Nord Béniguet**
BY

*Roc
du
Rouget*

Pte de Kermorvan
Fl.5s20m22M
Horn60s
Oc.G.4s

Le
Conquet

BYB

Red

BRB

La Vieille Noire
BYB

*Ile de
Béniguet*

**Ar Christian
Braz**
BYB

**Tournant et
Lochrist**
Iso.R.4s

Lochrist
DirOc(3)12s49m22M

Fornic
YBY

Green White

145°

W △△ W

Saint-Mathieu
Fl.15s56m29M
& DirF.54m28M

Pte de
S-Mathieu

187°

*Roche du
Magellan*

Point du
Cormoran

55'

*Kervourok
(13)*

50

Men Civien
G

Fourmi

Les Vieux
Moines
Vis

Fl.R.4s16m5M
R

4°45'W

20'

(Oc(2)R.6s) and St Pierre then pass between Rouget (Fl.G.4s) and Gde Vinotière (LFl.R.10s15m5M). At this point the tide is at its strongest and the bottom is very uneven so rough conditions are common. With the help of the tide ground speed should be high and so the pain will be short-lived. Pass the Tournant et Lochrist (Iso.R.4s) and as you leave Les Vieux Moines (Fl.R.4s16m5M) to port you emerge into the relative calm and gentle tides of the Rade de Brest.

TOWARDS THE RAZ

From Pointe St Mathieu to the Raz is 15 miles. If you arrive at Pte St Mathieu at low water slack you have about 5 hours to cover that distance before the ebb starts (Brest -0045) at the Raz. This should be ample time in most conditions. The tides are weak and will be angled across, rather than directly opposing your track.

A yacht approaches La Valbelle buoy in perfect conditions in the Chenal du Four

The Four light Presqu'île St Laurent through the mist

At night One of the major difficulties of a night passage of the Four is that there are so many bright lights. It demands a clear head to be sure they are correctly identified. It is quite possible to buoy-hop but then the unlit St Pierre and Taboga buoys represent a significant hazard.

Using the backbearing of 070° on the Ile Vierge light as a clearing bearing for the inshore hazards, pass close south of the Grande Basse de Port-Sall W cardinal buoy. With this astern a course of 200° will carry you clear of the Le Four lighthouse. Hold this course until the directional light of the Chenal de l' Aberildut shows to port, by which time you should have identified the bright lights of Pte Kermorven (Fl.5s20m22M Horn 60s) and Pte St Mathieu (Fl.15s56m29M). Bring these into line (158°30´T) and you will enter the beam of the Pte St Mathieu directional light (DirF.54m28M). Stay in this beam until the Pte de Corsen light (Q.WRG.33m12-8M) goes green, then white. This white sector will guide you through the Rouget and Grande Vinotière buoys which should be visible ahead. As you pass the Tournant et Lochrist buoy the Pte St Mathieu sectored light will change from

La Valbelle buoy. Beyond, Les Plaitresses beacon stands white against the sky

red to white. Turn towards the light in the white sector. The intense white sector of the Trezien light gives an exit bearing from astern but in practice the Les Vieux Moines (Fl.R.4s16m5M) beacon is easier to use. Once it is obscured turn back into its visible red sector and leave the beacon to port.

Les Vieux Moines near low tide. Beyond is Pointe St Mathieu, its two lighthouses seeming to sprout from the monastic ruins

TOWARDS L'ABERWRAC'H

By day Pointe Saint Mathieu is easy to
identify, its lighthouse towers apparently
sprouting from the monastic ruins. Les
Vieux Moines beacon stands clear before
the point. Leaving Les Vieux Moines to
starboard will take you clear of the
inshore hazards to the south of Pointe St
Mathieu and from here the Tournant et
Lochrist buoy can be passed on either
hand. Rouget and Grande Vinotière
show up clearly off Pointe Kermorven.
Using the transit astern of Pte St
Mathieu and Pte Kermorven as a
reference, pass from buoy to buoy to La
Valbelle, reversing the southward courses
to L'AberWrac'h and the Channel.

At night Approach the all-round white of
Pte St Mathieu (Fl.15s56m29M), leave
Les Vieux Moines to starboard and
continue on a heading of approximately
225° until the Pte St Mathieu sectored
light shows green then white. You should
leave the intense sector of the Trezien
light as Tournant et Lochrist falls astern.
Now either turn directly for Rouget and
Grande Vinotière or wait until you enter
the white sector of the Pte Corsen light.
Once Pte St Mathieu is in line this transit
astern will guide you to La Valbelle and
open water.

HARBOURS AND ANCHORAGES

Anse de Bertheaume

Coming from the Raz de Sein it is
possible that you will arrive too early.
Temporary anchorage may be had in
Anse de Bertheaume with good shelter
from the north and west. Give a good
offing to the SW corner of the bay as Le
Chat is a reef that extends 250m from
the shore below the fort. Anchor NE of
Le Chat. Some supplies in the village
nearby.

Brest (Moulin Blanc)

There are several good anchorages in the Rade de Brest. The marina is at Moulin Blanc. There are only basic supplies nearby and it is about 2km from the city but there is a regular bus service which passes a large supermarket. There are bars and restaurants at the marina and it is well serviced for repairs and chandlery. Brest is a large, historic city with many features worth visiting. Entry to Moulin Blanc is from the Goulet de Brest and is well marked. A buoyed channel leads to the marina. Visitors' berths are located in the northern half of the marina.

Le Conquet

A small harbour mostly filled with resident moorings, which is also busy with the ferry service to Ile de Sein. Space for visitors is limited but it is a pretty little place with good bars and restaurants. If on arriving at the southern end of the Chenal du Four you think better of it, Le Conquet is convenient to await better conditions.

L'Aberlldut

Entry is between reefs extending from the shore. Pass south of the port-hand beacon Le Lieu with the church spires Lanildut and Brélès in line (079°) before joining the channel marked with small port-hand beacons. At night a sectored light (DirOc(2)WR.6s12m25/20M) marks the entrance. The inlet is a centre for harvesting seaweed and can be less than fragrant at low water. Space for

Pointe Kermorven's square lighthouse is unmistakable

PIPER'S EXPERIENCE CHENAL DU FOUR

Southward

Visibility in L'AberWrac'h was poor in the early morning. Banks of fog drifted across the estuary and the rising sun was seen as a pallid disc above the grey veil. It was a hard decision to make, but early fog is common on this coast and I was sure it would burn off as the sun got higher. I dropped the mooring and motored down the river. Passing Ile Corsen I was reassured by the sight of the pencil tower of the Ile Vierge lighthouse, four miles away to the north. There was little wind, but out in the open sea a light northerly ruffled the water as we passed the Levanter buoy at the entrance to the Grand Chenal. A swell rose and fell among the rocks to port, marked by the La Petite Fourche N cardinal. There are three in sight from here around the entrance to L'Aber Benoit so it's important to know which one you're looking at. The last of the flood was pushing its way eastwards.

Gradually the fog gave way to sullen haze and the sun faded from view beyond a leaden sky, yet from landward a golden glow hinted that the people ashore were having a brighter day than us mariners. The Corn Carhai beacon showed up in silhouette, marking the rocks off Port-Sall

which stood black against the light. An uncomfortable sea heaved in irregular rhythms below our keel and off the starboard bow the Grande Basse de Port-Sall W cardinal buoy rose and fell as the hills and valleys formed and reformed beneath it. I sheeted the main flat against the roll, which damped the motion somewhat, but the breath of air from the north was hardly enough to keep the sail filled as *Piper* rolled to port.

There seems to be an inshore set to the tide here. I watched closely my bearing on the Basse Paupian W cardinal buoy. Rounding it I swung *Piper* down towards the Chenal du Four and the swell came in from astern. We were accelerating on the tide now and the seas diminished rapidly. The rectangular shape of the Four lighthouse showed through the haze, a small motor fishing boat buzzing around its base.

With the tide, the squared off main and poled out genoa *Piper* was making good enough speed to be well past Pointe de St Mathieu before the turn. I cut the engine, glad of the peace. As we drew abeam of L'Aberildut a gun fired inshore – the start of a race – and the fleet poured out of the channel. Rounding the outer mark, they turned downwind and one by one the spinnakers burst into colourful bloom. The practised efficiency of the crews as the sails were hoist and set was a pleasure to watch.

From Le Four to La Valbelle is five miles. I could make out the large red beacon and the white of Les Plaitresses to its right, relieved that my confidence in the visibility had been vindicated. On the chart this gap looks a small target to hit in poor visibility. In reality it's over half a mile. The channel looks very complicated as charted but in good visibility and daylight it is very easy. Under a sky clearing from grey to blue *Piper* and I were content to buoy hop down to Pointe St Mathieu with the back markers of the racing fleet for company as we rounded Les Vieux Moines.

Northward

Piper and I beat out of Douarnenez in a brisk westerly, laying Morgat on the first tack. With the Cap de la Chèvre to windward the next tack was drier but then it was back to flying spray as we worked around to weather the point. The wind was veering and instead of our intended direct tack to Pointe de Saint Mathieu we were forced to go deep into Anse de Dinan, weathering the Tas de Pois before taking a northerly tack through the Chenal de Grand Leac'h. We held this tack until under the shelter of Anse de Bertheaume.

The tide was already running strongly when we reached Pointe de Saint Mathieu and we had been sailing hard to windward for nearly eight hours. For a minute or two I thought about going into Le

Conquêt. The seas were short and breaking and the motion so violent that I didn't have a hand free for the camera. I was on the point of giving in when a wave hit *Piper's* weather bow, went straight into the air and hit me full in the face. I glowered into the wind, spat the salt from my mouth and wiped my eyes with my hand.

'Right then you b*gger! We're coming through.'

I left the reef in the main but unrolled the genoa a turn or two, sheeted it hard and let *Piper* do her best work. Spray and green water flew aft and I stood ankle deep in the cockpit with both hands on the tiller, singing *The Bonnie Ship the Diamond* at the top of my lungs.

Sailing slightly free, our course took us inshore and we tacked westwards north of St Pierre starboard-hand buoy. North again, then another tack lined us up with La Valbelle and Les Plaitresses. Our next tack would now clear Le Four and we would be freed off with every mile northward, but as we left the shelter of the reefs and islands of Ouessant the sea mounted. At the same time the wind decreased so that by the time we passed Port-Sall it was down to Force 2. I shook out all the reefs and sheeted the main flat.

Our northward passage of the Chenal du Four ended as the southward had begun, rolling in a lumpy sea. With *Piper* secured to a mooring in L'AberWrac'h I treated myself to dry clothes, a hot camembert baguette and a mug of hot chocolate. Soon I was fast asleep with my head on the chart table and the mug still in my hand.

L'Aberlldut at sunset. There is depth to anchor here now as a result of sand dredging, but the smell of the harvested seaweed can be a little strong

visitors is constricted by these activities and by moorings of resident craft. The removal of sand for agricultural and building use has resulted in an increase in depths throughout the inlet. Ashore there are small shops, a café and a post office in the village.

L'AberWrac'h

L'AberWrac'h is a convenient landfall from across the Channel. The harbour is a popular yachting centre and home to a sailing school. The entrances to the estuary are well marked; the easiest for a first-time visitor is the Grand Chenal, marked at its western entrance by the Libenter buoy. Approaching from any direction the Ile Vierge lighthouse is an unmistakable mark. There are marina facilities, pontoon berths and visitors'' moorings at La Pelue. Ashore there is a lively selection of bars and restaurants. Except at the Friday morning market there are no supplies available, the nearest being 2km by road at Landéda. Here there are banks, post office and a variety of small village shops.

CHARTS AND PILOTS

Imray C35, C36
Admiralty 1432, 3345, 2694
SHOM 7094, 7122
The Shell Channel Pilot Tom Cunliffe
    (Imray)
North Brittany and the Channel Islands
    RCC Pilotage Foundation/John
    Lawson (Imray)
Secret Anchorages of Brittany Peter
    Cumberlidge (Imray)

7. CHICHESTER BAR

Chichester Harbour encloses a huge area of sheltered water with 17 miles of navigable channels, home to over 10,000 boats of all shapes and sizes. All this water and all these boats must enter or leave through one narrow channel and to reach the sea they must pass Chichester Bar.

The Bar has a nasty reputation locally, but, as harbourmaster John Davis says:

'If you choose your conditions and time of tide it is nothing that a competent mariner should fear.'

Yet yachts do get caught out. In 2001 Hayling Island LB had callouts to around 15 incidents attributable to the Bar. Is this number of incidents due to the nature of the bar or is it more a function of the law of averages given the high volume of traffic, much of it coming from very sheltered waters to meet the open sea in this narrow channel?

'Chichester Bar is a pussy-cat when you get it right but a bastard when you get it wrong. We left Chichester Marina at 0600 to cross the bar at about high water

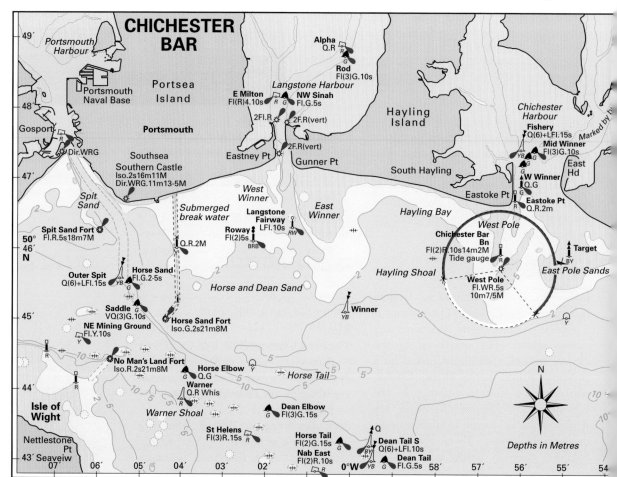

to head through the Looe channel and it was easy. On the VHF, we heard the lifeboat being called to somebody who had gone aground an hour or so later. The channel is well buoyed to the bar coming out but not so easy going in. There are a couple of patches which could cause a problem.'

Brendan Chandler
Leaving Chichester on a delivery
to the east coast

AVOIDING THE PROBLEMS

Heading outwards, Chichester's sheltered water may give little real idea of what conditions are like outside or at the Bar. Log on to www.chimet.co.uk before you leave home. This gives wind speed and direction including the strongest gust, plus detailed conditions of sea and tide. The data is recorded at Chichester Bar beacon and so is a very real picture of sea conditions you will encounter should you venture outside.

Smoothest conditions will be found within an hour of high water. If there is anything of a southerly wind a departure against the last of the flood will avoid the worst of the seas at the Bar. It could make punching a foul tide all the way down from your berth worth the effort. Nick Rizzi, owner of Sparkes Yacht Harbour, advises:

'Don't go on the last two hours of the ebb. The rest of the time it's not a real problem.'

GETTING IN

Approaching from the east stay well out of Bracklesham Bay, turning for the West Pole beacon when the Eastoke beacon is just open to the east of it. From the west a back-bearing on Horse Sand fort of 260° will clear the shoals, once past the Winner S cardinal and will take you to the West Pole beacon.

From the south make for a point about 100 metres east of West Pole beacon. Resist the temptation to cut close to the beacon, holding out about 100 metres to the east where you will find the deepest water. The waypoint recommended in 2003 Chichester Harbour news is 50°45′.32N 00°56′.60W (WGS 84). The latest waypoint position can be found on the Chichester Harbour Conservancy website. From there a track of 013° will take you clear of the shoals and safely into the deeper water off Eastoke Point. Avoid going too close inshore here, to avoid the groynes protruding from the beach. Their ends are marked by small red posts.

Between the West Winner beacon and the Northwest Winner buoy both shores are steep-to and clean so it is possible to use the full width of the channel. By the same token, the sands of the Winner shoal very quickly once you cross east of a line between the West and Northwest Winner. Once level with the North Winner you are safely inside Chichester Harbour and can turn to port for Sparkes Yacht Harbour, starboard for Itchenor and Thorney channels or straight ahead for Emsworth.

In the spring of 2002 the Bar was dredged to a least depth of 1.5 metres. Chichester Harbour handbook contains a

Horse Sand Fort. A back bearing of 260° is a useful guide for an approach from the west

The Winner S cardinal buoy

Eastoke beacon and the clubhouse and boatyard buildings beyond

diagram of the most recent survey of the bar and where to find the deepest water.

One cause of trouble is that skippers arriving back late at the end of a weekend are tempted to push their luck in an attempt to get back to their own berth. This temptation is understandable given the likely cost and inconvenience of finding temporary alternative berthing in the Solent. Solent Coastguard confirmed that the end of weekend rush on a spring tide is the peak time for mishaps. Yachts cutting the corner, or just being crowded by the volume of traffic, find themselves aground. The safest way in is to give yourself plenty of time and stick to the recommended track.

A combination of a fresh southerly wind facing a strong ebb is always a recipe for unpleasant conditions and

White water on the shallows to seaward of the East Head buoy, but in the Chichester Channel the water is smooth

steep standing waves can develop very quickly in the entrance. With the Isle of Wight standing in the way of SW winds one would expect a little shelter from this quarter, but the entrance to Chichester can fall within the stronger, more turbulent conditions of the airflow disturbed by the island. If you're late and trying to enter against the ebb, with ground speed reduced to almost nothing the pain can last a long time. A better alternative could be to seek a sheltered anchorage close in the lee of the Isle of Wight and wait for the next tide.

'The answer is common sense and due prudence and do your arithmetic.'

Lt Col John Q Davis RM
Chichester Harbourmaster

Abeam of Eastoke Beacon. With wind and tide together conditions are benign

Spray flying as *Piper* meets the steep seas in wind over tide conditions at Chichester Bar

HARBOURS AND ANCHORAGES

Once in through Chichester Bar there are several options:

Hayling Island

Sparkes Marina is the nearest berthing to the entrance. A dredged (2m) channel leads from its entrance at Black Point, and around Sandy Point. Pass to the south of the E cardinal beacon and follow the X shaped transit markers into the channel between red and green posts to the marina.

Facilities Showers, laundry, chandlery, bar-restaurant, limited provisions, fuel, repairs.

Itchenor Reach

Itchenor Pool
Visitors' moorings and a floating pontoon are available off Itchenor. Chichester Harbourmaster's office is ashore by the ferry landing. A water taxi operates between the moorings and the jetty. There are no supplies available here but the Ship Inn has a good reputation for food.

PIPER'S EXPERIENCE CHICHESTER BAR

Piper had spent the night at Yarmouth and with a fresh southerly breeze set sail for Chichester. Conditions were sufficiently fresh for me to appreciate the protection of land to windward and I decided to stay under the lee of the Isle of Wight until No Man's Land Fort forced us offshore. Leaving the shelter I set a course to pass close to the south of the Winner buoy, cutting across the edge of the Horse and Dean Sand. Still two miles distant, the West Pole was difficult to make out. I used the back bearing on Horse Sand Fort of 260° as a clearing bearing to keep us out of the shallows until I had identified the West Pole. Despite the strength of the wind the seas were slight.

At last I made out the West Pole beacon but beyond it the entrance was still very indistinct, a seemingly continuous line of golden sand stretching across the shoreward horizon, smudged by the summer haze. It was 1hr before HW Portsmouth. In the absence of a distinct channel the temptation was to make for a point close to the beacon, barely visible against the beach clutter, but the deepest water is to be found about 100 metres east

of the beacon. I checked the GPS and held my course. From the waypoint we swept in through the narrows. I held Piper to a nominal track of 013° but in the strong current this was at best an approximation. Shallow water showed clearly to starboard and as we passed the North Winner and rounded the bend in the channel there was the usual buzz of anticipation of making our first entrance of an unfamiliar harbour. On the whole things went quite smoothly and as we rounded the Mid Winner and made for Itchenor the water became glassy smooth in the lee of the banks.

The tide which had swept us up the Itchenor Reach was easing, which made an easy job of coming alongside and tying up on the visitors' pontoon.

I spent a pleasant couple of hours in Itchenor and by the time I was ready to leave the tide was ebbing strongly. The wind was still fresh but had now veered a little, blowing from SW at about Force 5. Inside the harbour the air was warm and mild and the water rippled pleasantly as we passed Deep End. A short sea was running in the Chichester Channel as we beat down past the Camber but this did no more than throw spray across Piper's foredeck. The water was smooth once more for the long tack between East Head and the Mid Winner. In order

to sail as free as possible through the narrows I held the westerly course, tacking when I dared go no closer to the Hayling Island shore. Through the narrows a nasty chop was running. Piper's low foredeck was soon awash but her long keel and fine lines served us well and she ploughed on willingly. The sea was smoother closer to the Hayling Island shore but even with Piper close hauled our course took us out towards the shallows.

Piper answered well but the seas were now running at about 4ft high and very steep. It was a wet and uncomfortable ride and I had to judge carefully the right moment to bring Piper's head through the wind. A missed tack could have had us on the shingle.

Astern of us a larger, modern yacht was making heavy weather of it, showing us her keel at regular intervals. Just past the West Winner beacon I hove-to to let her catch up so I could get a photograph. Having got my picture I put in a tack towards Eastoke Point to keep us in deeper water. The larger yacht thought better of it and turned back inside. Piper ploughed on. Though the westward tacks were short in the narrow channel, the run of the tide lifted us well up to windward. Conditions continued choppy until we were well clear of the entrance, seeming at their worst as we approached the

Bar beacon. The wind now appeared to veer so that had we been able to hold our open water course through the narrows it would have taken us through the Bar on one tack. I suspect that the land close on either hand deflected the wind to follow the channel and so headed Piper as she made for sea. As it was, we now had a long beat down the Solent.

Chichester Yacht Basin

A modern, well serviced marina. Showers, launderette. Fuel, water and supplies are available. Engineers, sailmaker, rigging, chandler on site. Chichester Yacht Club is very welcoming to visiting yachts' crews. Access to the marina is via a lock HW±0400. Light signals on lock: Red = wait, Green = enter.

Birdham Pool

Set in a delightful location, services include showers, toilets, a fully equipped shipyard, electrical engineer, chandler, sailmaker. However, there are no shops close by.

Approaches dry 1m so a rising tide is preferable, otherwise proceed with caution. Access to the marina is via a lock HW±0300 for 0700 to 2200 during the season.

Bosham anchoring prohibited and no facilities for visitors. All moorings private.

Anchoring is possible in the channel south of Cobnor Point. A ball must be displayed by day and an anchor light at night.

Thorney Channel

Anchorage off Pilsley Island.

Emsworth

Emsworth Yacht Harbour has a sill which dries 2.4m. There is limited space for visitors.

Northney

Northney Yacht Harbour has a sill which dries at chart datum. There is usually space for visitors.

USEFUL CONTACTS

Chichester Harbour Office
☎ 01243 512301
Email harbourmaster@conservancy.co.uk
www.conservancy.co.uk
VHF Ch 16, 14 Call *Chichester Harbour Radio* or *Chichester*

Harbour Patrol (during office hours and when conservancy vessels are manned)
Coastguard, Lee on Solent
☎ 023 9255 2100
Weather information: www.chimet.co.uk
Weathercall ☎ 09068 22645
Sparkes Yacht Harbour
☎ 02392 463572 VHF Ch 37
Chichester Marina
☎ 01243 512731 VHF Ch 80
Birdham Pool Marina ☎ 01243 512310
Northney Marina ☎ 02392 466321
VHF Ch 80
Emsworth Marina ☎ 01243 377727
VHF Ch 37 or 80

CHARTS AND PILOTS

Imray C9, 2200.4
The Shell Channel Pilot Tom Cunliffe (Imray)

A yacht approaching Eastoke Beacon as it leaves Chichester Harbour against the last of the flood

8. THE GULF OF CORRYVRECKAN AND THE NORTHERN CHANNELS OF THE SOUND OF JURA

The Gulf of Corryvreckan: the very name sounds ominous and threatening. Seasoned yachtsmen blanch at the thought of its infamous whirlpools and overfalls, 'big enough to swallow a trawler'. The name means Breacan's Cauldron, after a Pictish chieftain reputed to have drowned there. According to legend, its swirling depths are home to a huge sea monster. But how much of Corryvreckan's fearsome reputation is myth and how much is fact?

The Gulf of Corryvreckan lies at the northern tip of Jura, separating it from the island of Scarba. At the narrowest point it is about 0.6 miles wide and from east to west about 2 miles. Depths in mid-channel are around 100 metres but the bottom is very uneven. Near the eastern end there is a hole with a depth of 219 metres, big enough to swallow the Blackpool Tower, and towards the western end a shelf extends from the Scarba shore with a depth of 29 metres.

HOW THE TIDES WORK

The tidal range in the north of the Sound of Jura is a metre less than on the west side of the island, giving a half metre difference from west to east at high and low water. On the flood, the tide runs north up the Sound of Jura, gradually being constricted by the nearness of the Argyll shore to the islands. The other northern exits to the Sound of Jura, Cuan Sound and The Sound of Luing are relatively shallow, so the bulk of the water escapes through the deep channel of Corryvreckan. The uneven bottom causes turbulence throughout the flow, with powerful vertical currents sinking to or welling up from the depths to appear as huge blisters on the surface. Downstream of the 29-metre shelf a 4-metre high standing wave develops. This height can be doubled by westerly wind or swell and its roar can be heard six miles away in Crinan. On the Jura side, north of Carraig Mhor another overfall can form. In certain conditions these can join to form a solid wall of water right across the Gulf. On the ebb the flow is slightly calmer and there is slightly less turbulence at the 29m shelf as its westerly side is not as steep as the east. Close to both shores reverse eddies form, running as strongly as the main flow, and whirlpools can be created at the boundaries between currents.

Unintentional passages of the gulf have happened as unwary yachts venture too near the powerful currents that sweep from Loch Shuna through the narrow space between Jura and Scarba. Motoring flat out, they are drawn irresistibly backwards into the dreaded Gulf as they fight a losing battle with 8 knots of tide. Despite all this Clyde Coastguard revealed that there are in fact very few incidents requiring assistance in Corryvreckan. The officer I spoke to could remember none in the past six years but acknowledged that perhaps this is because its reputation keeps sailors at a respectful distance.

Alistair lives and works at Craobh, just across from the Gulf.

'I set off down to Crinan in a boat when I first came up here. The tide got a grip of us and I went through Corryvreckan.

I anchored in the bay behind Eilean Beag and waited 'til the tide turned then came back.'

He shrugs and grins ruefully:

'Ignorance is bliss. I was just lucky that conditions were perfect. It was a great place for a picnic, though, I found that out.'

Another of Corryvreckan's near-victims was George Orwell, seized by the Gulf's current aboard a small boat whilst staying on Jura when he was writing *1984.*

Despite all the horror stories, in the right conditions yachts regularly pass through without trouble.

This is the experience of the yacht *Alert* heading south:

'Gently motoring with hardly any wind at all, picking our way through the islands we arrived off the West Coast of Scarba. Still gently motoring about 4 knots [our skipper] announced that we were going through the Gulf of Corryvreckan, the notorious whirlpool and the swallower-up of boats. All pilot books say avoid the gulf so that must be why he decided to take us through. After all the stories it was somewhat of an anti-climax but nevertheless possibly a worthwhile experience.'

A SAFE PASSAGE: THE KEY

A safe passage can be made at slack water in calm conditions, but any westerly wind or swell can create appalling conditions when meeting the flood

Slack water varies from 1¾ hrs before high and low water Oban at springs to 1 hour before at neaps.

Making a passage eastwards with the first of the ebb it is a mistake to arrive too early as it will be impossible to make headway and there will still be rough water around the Great Race. The western entrance will usually calm down very quickly as the ebb begins to run. To time your entrance accurately, temporary

Looking across Loch Shuna and the southern tip of Shuna to Corryvreckan. Calm conditions here may give no hint of what's happening to the west of the Gulf

The rocky shore of Scarba in the Gulf of Corryvreckan. Depths reach 100 metres quite close

The boundary between the main flow and the reverse eddy close to the Scarba shore

anchorage can be had to the south of the Gulf in Port nan Urrachann (56°10´.8N 05°44´.5W) on the west side of Jura or to the north in Bagh Uamh nan Giall (56° 07.4N 05° 45.3W) on the west side of Scarba.

On entering keep to a track just south of the mid-line of the Gulf and if making for Craobh turn to pass a cable or two off Rubha na Una before shaping a direct course for Loch Shuna.

On the flood the calmest water is found closer to the Jura shore. If heading north and making a passage at low water, be aware that the Great Race builds up very quickly as the flood gains strength. Getting across this can be a difficult judgement. The worst of the overfalls begin at the 29m shelf on the Scarba side, just across the Gulf from Eilean Beag. If it is already too rough to go northwards here the only alternative will be a long detour towards the northern tip of Colonsay.

Even in calm conditions beware of going through with the flood after periods of strong westerly weather. The calm of Loch Shuna will give no hint of the mayhem being caused by leftover swell at the other side of the Corryvreckan. By the time you find out, it may be impossible to turn back.

Pilot books are unanimous in their advice. Martyn Lawrence gives very detailed information about the Gulf but concludes:

'. . .the fundamental advice, especially to yachtsmen unfamiliar with the west coast, must be to avoid Corryvreckan and to avoid being drawn accidentally into it. . .'

GULF OF CORRYVRECKAN

Rubha na Faoilaig
Bàgh Gleann a Mhaoil
Rubha na Una
Scarba
Camas nam Bairneach
Rubha Righinn
To/from Craobh
Reverse eddy on flood
Gulf of Corryvreckan
To/from Dorus Mor
When heading North you must be clear of the Great Race before the flood is turning strongly
Eilean Mór
Eilean Beag
Buige Rk
Jura
Bàgh Gleann nam Muc
Depths in Metres
45'
44'
5°43'W
42'
41'

As the tide begins to run the turbulence is clearly visible on the surface

The edge of the 'whirlpool', really an upward vertical current. This is taken from the deck of Duncan Phillips' launch *Farsain*

Right on top of the 'whirlpool' the upward-welling water appears as blisters on the surface

The Grey Dogs (Little Corryvreckan).

Tides in Corryvreckan

At springs

Turns E (ebb begins) HW Oban −0145

Turns west (flood begins)
HW Oban +0430

Spring rate 8kn

At neaps

Turns E HW Oban −0100

Turns W HW Oban +0515

AVOIDING THE GULF

Heading north from Islay a good plan is to pass up the Sound of Islay with a stopover at Colonsay or West Loch Tarbert on Jura. Then, continuing north on a fair tide, the flood is running out of Corryvreckan as you pass. With westerly weather or swell the Great Race extends several miles out from the gulf and a good offing is essential, perhaps as far west as Colonsay. Conversely, heading south, enter the Sound of Jura via Cuan Sound and Loch Shuna or the Sound of Luing and with a fair tide to carry you down the Sound of Jura you will pass Corryvreckan with the ebb running towards you, keeping you clear of its fearsome grip.

When making a northward passage up the Sound of Jura keep well to the east. Currents are strong throughout the area west of Reisa mhic Phaidean. The preferred track is east of Ruadh Sgeir continuing via Dorus Mhor and east of Reisa mhic Phaidean. Dorus Mhor has a fearsome reputation of its own and Loch Crinan is a useful stopover to await suitable conditions to continue.

ALTERNATIVES TO CORRYVRECKAN

Cuan Sound

Cuan Sound is the northernmost gateway to the Sound of Jura. In contrast with the Gulf of Corryvreckan its waters are shallow and the sound makes sudden changes of direction within its narrow channel. At the apex of its V-shaped course the Cleit Rock stands out into the flow, creating turbulence and eddies that make steering a straight course difficult. Cuan Sound demands careful pilotage and a quick hand on the helm. A passage through is always an intense experience.

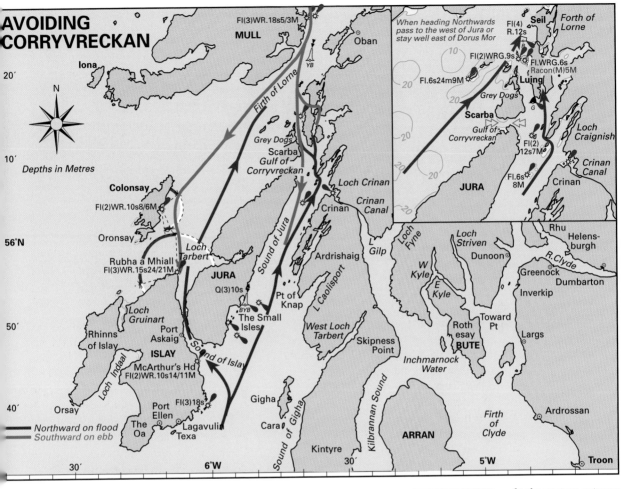

AVOIDING CORRYVRECKAN

Depths in Metres

20′

10′

56°N

50′

40′

Iona

MULL

Oban

FI(3)WR.18s5/3M

Firth of Lorne

Grey Dogs

Scarba

Gulf of Corryvreckan

Colonsay

FI(2)WR.10s8/6M

Oronsay

Rubha a Mhiall
FI(3)WR.15s24/21M

Loch Tarbert

JURA

Q(3)10s

Sound of Jura

Loch Crinan

Crinan

Crinan Canal

Ardrishaig

L Gilp

Loch Fyne

Rhu Helensburgh

Loch Striven

Dunoon

W Kyle

E Kyle

R.Clyde

Greenock

Dumbarton

Inverkip

Largs

Pt of Knap

BYB

The Small Isles

L Caolisport

West Loch Tarbert

Skipness Point

Roth esay

BUTE

Toward Pt

Loch Gruinart

Port Askaig

ISLAY

McArthur's Hd
FI(2)WR.10s14/11M

Sound of Islay

Rhinns of Islay

Loch Indaal

Orsay

Port Ellen

FI(3)18s

Lagavulin

Texa

The Oa

Gigha

Cara

Sound of Gigha

Kintyre

Kilbrannan Sound

Inchmarnock Water

ARRAN

Firth of Clyde

Ardrossan

Troon

30′

6°W

30′

5°W

Northward on flood
Southward on ebb

Inset:
When heading Northwards pass to the west of Jura or stay well east of Dorus Mor

Seil

Forth of Lorne

FI(4) R.12s

FI(2)WRG.9s

FI.WRG.6s
Racon(M)5M

FI.6s24m9M

Luing

Grey Dogs

Scarba

Gulf of Corryvreckan

JURA

FI(2) 12s7M

FI.6s 8M

Crinan

Loch Craignish

Crinan Canal

At the western entrance to Cuan Sound the pylons carrying power lines are an excellent mark

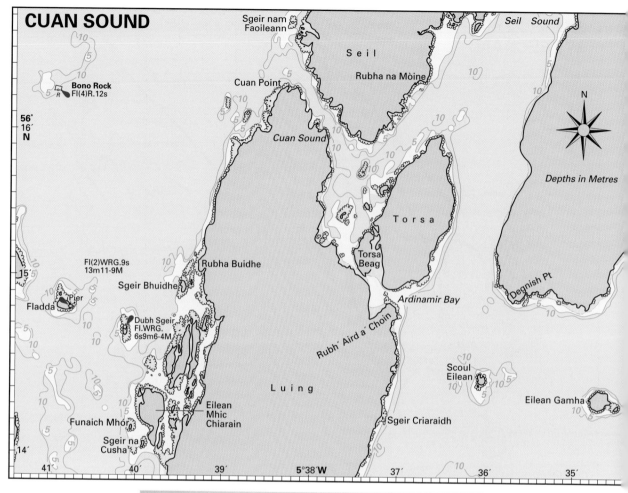

CUAN SOUND

Sgeir nam
Faoileann

Seil Sound

S e i l

Rubha na Mòine

Cuan Point

56°
16′
N

Cuan Sound

Bono Rock
Fl(4)R.12s

Depths in Metres

N

Torsa

Torsa
Beag

15′

Fl(2)WRG.9s
13m11-9M

Rubha Buidhe

Ardinamir Bay

Sgeir Bhuidhe

Degnish Pt

Pier

Dubh Sgeir
Fl.WRG.
6s9m6-4M

Fladda

Rubh′ Aird a′ Choin

Scoul
Eilean

L u i n g

Eilean Gamha

Funaich Mhòr

Eilean
Mhic
Chiarain

Sgeir Criaraidh

Sgeir na
Cusha

14′

41′   40′   39′   5°38′W   37′   36′   35′

The flood sweeping round
the Cleit Rock

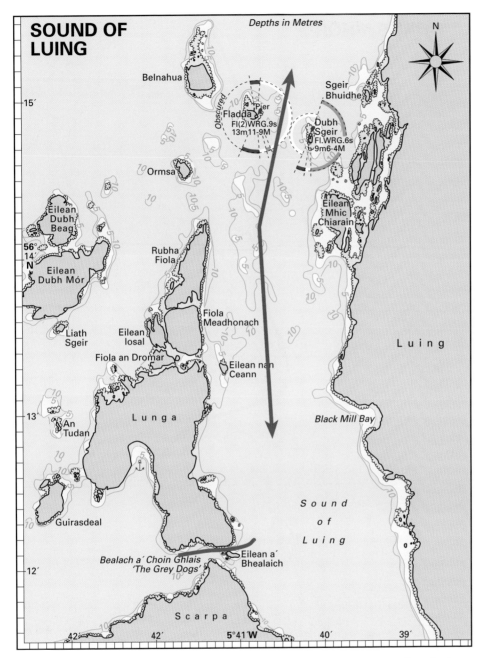

SOUND OF LUING

Depths in Metres

N

Belnahua

Sgeir Bhuidhe

15′

Obscured

Fladda
Fl(2) WRG.9s
13m 11-9M

Pier

Dubh Sgeir
Fl.WRG.6s
9m 6-4M

Ormsa

Eilean Mhic Chiarain

Eilean Dubh Beag

56°
14′
N

Rubha Fiola

Eilean Dubh Mór

L u i n g

Liath Sgeir

Eilean Iosal

Fiola Meadhonach

Fiola an Dromar

Eilean nan Ceann

13′

An Tudan

L u n g a

Black Mill Bay

S o u n d

o f

L u i n g

Guirasdeal

12′

Bealach a′ Choin Ghlais
'The Grey Dogs'

Eilean a′ Bhealaich

S c a r p a

42′   42′   5°41′W   40′   39′

Slack water is short-lived and the spring rate of 7 knots is attained very soon after the turn. Making the passage for the first time it is essential to have all the pilotage information rehearsed and ready to hand. Once you are into the grip of the tide there will be no turning back and little time to start reading the pilot book.

Passing westwards out of Loch Shuna beware of two submerged rocks just north of Torsa, the northernmost is about 2½ cables north of the island. Either pass within half a cable of the shore or give a good 3 cables offing. A clearing bearing of 290° on Rubha na Moine on the east shore of Seil island will see you safely

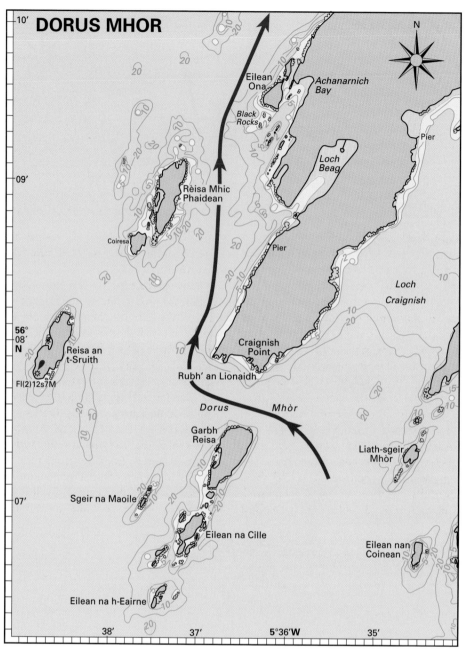

past, turning into the sound when the Cleit Rock is lined up in mid-channel. A reef extends from the southernmost tip of Seil Island so as you pass the Cleit Rock stay south of the mid-point of the channel.

Duncan Phillips assures me that it is very hard to hit the Cleit Rock, due to the tide pushing the boat's head away before you make contact. He demonstrated this during our trip aboard his launch and it certainly seemed to be true, but it is not an experiment I would care to repeat with *Piper*.

Once past the Cleit Rock line up in mid-channel and stay in the mid-stream

until north of Cuan Point. From here a turn westwards will avoid a rock due north of Cuan Point and about a cable from the west shore of Seil Island.

One advantage of Cuan Sound is that within its narrow confines it is sheltered from the weather and a passage can often be made here when other routes are untenable. With strong westerly weather against the flood, overfalls may be experienced at the western end. These are at their most severe over a rock ledge that extends southwards from the western shore of Seil island to about 2 cables northwest of Cuan Point. In turning to the southwest to avoid these overfalls beware of a drying rock Culanach about 3 cables slightly south of

west from Cuan Point. A course no further south than 260° will take you clear of this.

Passing eastwards through Cuan Sound the pylons are a good mark to identify the entrance, although in certain conditions of light they too can be hard to spot. Approaching from the north you may find the rock a cable off the Seil shore. Stay a couple of cables off until the sound is fully open. Under the pylons stay in mid-channel, making directly for the beacon on the Cleit Rock. At what seems like the last minute (in reality about 50 metres from the rock) turn to pass to the north of it, staying south of the mid-point of the channel. On leaving the sound either continue northwards

Turbulence in the Dorus Mhor at the boundary between contrary flows

The difference in water level between east and west is clearly visible in the Grey Dogs

**Fladda Lighthouse.
Sound of Luing**

until abeam of Rubha na Moine before turning into Loch Shuna or stay within 50 metres of the Torsa shore to avoid the rocks to the north of the island.

The Sound of Luing

Broad and very shallow in its northern part, the Sound of Luing is the most straightforward of the passages. One submerged rock, 2 cables northeast of the little islet of Funaich Mhor, is easily avoided. Making a northward passage there is the additional risk of being drawn into Corryvreckan, but an approach from Craobh or from Dorus Mhor and north of Hutcheson Rock takes you clear of this arm of the tide. Once in the sound stay in mid-channel until north of Lunga then approach the Fladda lighthouse on a bearing of 355°, then abeam of Ormsa turn to pass midway between Fladda and Dubh Sgeir. The southbound passage is an exact reversal.

With streams of 7.5 kn the sound can be very rough in conditions of wind over

The enclosed waters of Puilladobhrain, with cloud covering the hills of Mull

tide, especially in the shallow northern section where the bottom is very uneven and at the sudden change in depth that occurs between Eilean nan Ceann and Rubha na lic. In these conditions Cuan Sound is to be preferred.

HARBOUR INFORMATION

CRAOBH HAVEN MARINA

Craobh Haven Marina is an artificial harbour built around the small islands off the once tiny hamlet of Craobh. Ashore the new development has been sympathetically laid out and, though modern, does not clash too harshly with its idyllic surroundings. Entrance is on the north side where a green buoy marks a rock. Within the marina a buoyed channel keeps you clear of a reef within the breakwater. The Lord of the Isles pub serves excellent food and there is a small bistro. There is a small general store but it's as well to be stocked up with major supplies. The boatyard has a travel-hoist, repair facilities and a chandlery. The marina has power and water alongside and there are showers, toilets and a launderette ashore. Diesel is available, but not petrol.

Contact
☎ 01852 500222
If you fancy a close look at the Corryvreckan, Duncan Phillips runs trips from Craobh through the gulf in his powerful launch *Farsain*, returning via the Grey Dogs (Little Corryvreckan), the Sound of Luing and Cuan Sound against the tide. ☎ 01852 500664

CHARTS AND PILOTS

Imray C65, 2800 series
Admiralty 2326
By far the most comprehensive information is given in
A Yachtsman's Guide to the Isle of Mull and Adjacent Coasts Martin Lawrence (Imray)

Tranquility in Craobh Haven, only a few miles from Corryvreckan and within earshot of its worst moods

PIPER'S EXPERIENCE – THE GULF OF CORRYVRECKAN

A brisk southerly, scudding low clouds and a fine drizzle accompanied *Piper* up from Craighouse. The prospects were not inviting and as we passed east of Ruadh Sgeir I was considering a stopover at Crinan. It got no worse, however, and with the fresh breeze and a fair tide I was soon lining *Piper* up with the Dorus Mhor. There was still an hour of the ebb to run and I was bracing myself for a shaking but as we approached I could see that conditions were smooth enough to see the direction of the currents. At the margins on either hand a strong back eddy was running and broken water showed where these opposing streams rubbed shoulders. We rounded Craignish Point, passing to the east of Reisa Mhic Phaidean. Somewhere ahead the Hutcheson Rock lay in wait, half submerged and ready to rip the bottom out of the careless. A clearing bearing astern (210°T) on the eastern edge of Reisa Mhic Phaidean provided a safe course and once we were abeam of the fortified hill of Druim a Achanarnich I was able to relax.

After a restful few days at Craobh, where *Piper* was hauled out for a minor repair we left Craobh an hour before the end of the ebb and motored in calm conditions towards Scarba to line up with the southern half of the Gulf. The sky was overcast, with dark clouds obscuring the tops of the Jura hills. In the dismal light the Gulf of Corryvreckan was a brooding presence. The previous day could not have been more different. Aboard Duncan Phillips' launch we had roared through the Gulf in bright sunshine. I had been relaxed and confident as with Duncan at the wheel we explored the eddies and whirlpools. Now I was alone and terrified. Despite the chill a trickle of sweat ran down my spine.

In my anxiety to 'get it over with' I had arrived a little early. The last of the ebb was still running as we approached the North of Jura and the current reduced our speed over the ground to less than one knot. All around us the water swirled and rippled. *Piper* was running on the spot.

At last, the surface of the water went smooth and still and we began to move forward. Slack water was very brief and as we passed abeam of the 29m shelf off Scarba ripples were forming on the surface on its seaward side. A hundred metres to starboard a disc of water seemed to rotate on the surface. The light, the solitude and the anxiety played tricks with my imagination. I felt like a player in a Homeric saga. Would tentacles reach from the deep to seize my little ship? The sight of a powerful launch astern brought me back to reality. Duncan was taking another group of clients through the Gulf.

I allowed the current to carry us to the west of Scarba and so clear of the back eddy which forms along its western shore, then turned northwards for the Garvellachs. *Piper* had passed safely through Breacan's Cauldron. In these conditions it was not a difficult passage and the pilotage in the broad channel much less demanding than the confines of Cuan Sound. Even so, it was with considerable relief that I headed *Piper* for the tamer waters of the Firth of Lorne.

The flood running through the Grey Dogs

9. JACK SOUND, RAMSEY SOUND AND THE BISHOPS

The great sweep of Cardigan Bay occupies most of the west coast of Wales. At the southern end of the bay the Pembroke peninsula stretches out westwards, narrowing the gap between Wales and Ireland and standing in the way of both boats and tides intent on passing through the St George's Channel. This, together with southwest winds and swell sweeping in from the Atlantic, make this an area to be taken seriously. The tide forces its way around and between the gathering of islands and

reefs dotted at the tip of the peninsula, and to pass between the Bristol Channel and Cardigan Bay boats must cope with the resulting strong streams, tide rips and overfalls.

THE CHOICE

For a yacht and crew capable of long passages the easiest way to deal with the St George's Channel is to keep well away from headlands and shipping lanes. The 180-mile direct passage between the

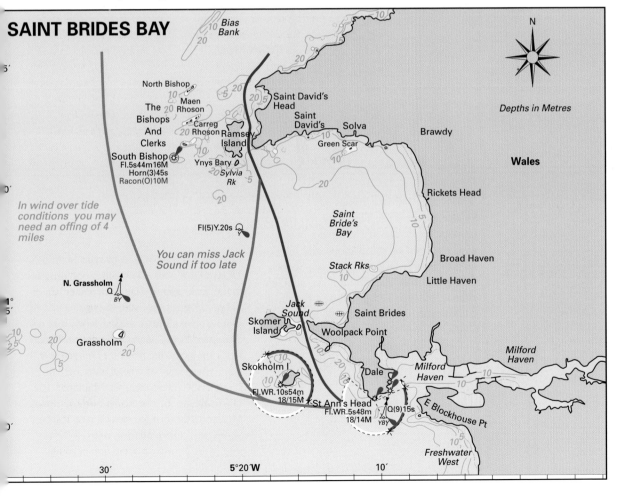

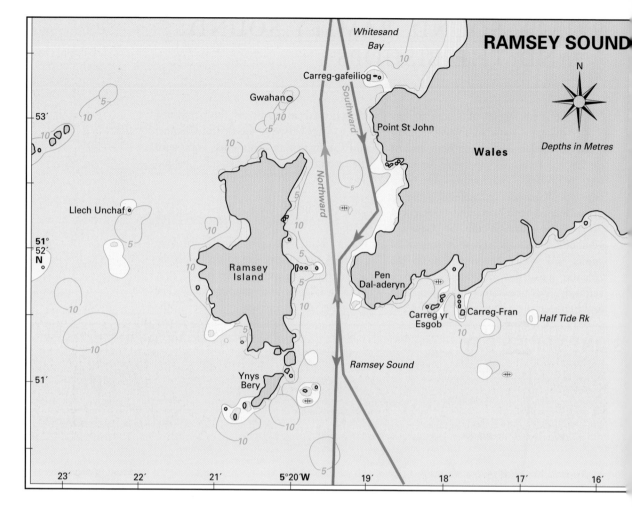

Scillies and Bardsey passes between the Smalls and its TSZ. The price you pay to keep passages shorter is to do business with the area of the Bishops and Clerks or go through Jack and Ramsey Sounds. Going outside the Bishops is simpler, although longer and not always the more comfortable option, especially in westerly winds.

Going through the sounds can be quicker and smoother but requires careful timing and pilotage.

GOING THROUGH

NORTHWARD

Leaving Milford Haven to pass St Anne's Head at LW will allow plenty of time to make Jack Sound for slack water there. From a position 100 metres east of Blackstones identify Tuskar Rock just off Wooltack Point. Make directly for Tuskar Rock on a bearing of 018°. This track will take you clear of the Cable off Anvil Point and Crabstones off Mainland Isle. Once abeam of the northernmost tip of Midland Isle turn for clear water. Ramsey Sound is 7 miles bearing 340°.

Approaching Ramsey Sound the Bitches can be seen extending from the shore of Ramsey Island. Steer for the middle of the gap between the outer end of the Bitches and the mainland shore. Once past the Bitches make for the tip of Ramsey Island at Trwyn Ogof Hen to avoid Horse Rock but beware of being drawn into the strong reverse eddy setting towards the island just north of the Bitches.

In wind over tide, rough water will also be found between Ramsey Island and Point St John. Smoother water will be found by keeping towards Gwahan, an isolated rock 300 metres north of the island, before setting a course for St David's Head.

SOUTHWARD

Leaving Fishguard, allowance must be made for the contrary tide which will be encountered during the 15 miles to St David's Head. Ramsey Sound opens as St David's Head is rounded. Approach Point St John on a SSE track to avoid the reef Carreg Gafeiliog then maintain 100 metres from the mainland shore, passing east of Horse Rock. Once past the Bitches maintain a southerly track to avoid Shoe Rock (dries 3.0m) 100 metres south of Pen Dal-aderyn.

Having passed through Ramsey Sound at slack water it is 7 miles to Jack Sound where, at springs, the tide has already been running for an hour. From 100 metres west of Tuskar Rock make for a point 100 metres east of Blackstones. The roughest water is to be found on the

South Bishop light beyond Meini Duon, a rocky islet off Ynys Bery

St Anne's Head at the entrance to Milford Haven

mainland side of the sound but to avoid the Crabstones (dries 3.7m) which will probably be just covered, beware of going west of this line. On the mainland side beware of the Cable, (dries 2.4m) 200m NW of the Anvil. With wind against tide there will be rough water on the windward side of the Sound. In southerlies this will be between Blackstones and Limpet Rocks. Smoother water will be found nearer to the Blackstones. Once south of the Bench the coast is steep-to round to St Anne's Head.

'*Wind against tide gives you the feeling that you're through the sounds, and then it suddenly hits you, you're not.*'

Jonathan Williams *Nimrod of Beaulieu*

In conditions of wind over a spring tide, or in any doubt, it is possible to miss Jack Sound by passing outside Skomer and Skokholm Islands, giving them an offing of at least 2 miles.

Jonathan has safely sailed through Jack and Ramsey Sound many times aboard his Dufour 35 *Nimrod of Beaulieu* A close friend of his father's was not so lucky. Delivering a 36´ steel ketch, they attempted to pass through Jack Sound without detailed charts. It was a perfect day and they just thought they would 'have a look'. A close encounter with what was probably the Crabstone almost resulted in the loss of the vessel.

Tides
Jack Sound
LW slack (north-going begins)
Springs: HW Milford Haven -0425 (Dover +0300) Max rate 7kn
Neaps: HW Milford Haven -0300 (Dover +0335) Max rate 5kn
HW slack (south-going begins)
Springs: HW Milford Haven +0200 (Dover -0300)
Neaps: HW Milford Haven +0300 (Dover -0400)

Ramsey Sound
LW slack
HW Milford Haven -0325 (Dover +0400) Max sp rate 6kn
HW slack
HW Milford Haven +0300 (Dover -0200) Max sp rate 6kn

Left Blackstones
Centre Mew Stone

Bishops

South-going (ebb) begins
Milford Haven +0500 (HW Dover)
North-going (flood) begins
Milford Haven –0125 (Dover +0600)

GOING AROUND

There are good harbours both north and south of the area: Fishguard in Cardigan Bay and Milford Haven around to the south at the entrance to the Bristol Channel. Both can be entered in all states of the tide and in rough weather. For a passage northwards, take the last of the ebb out of the Bristol Channel to arrive just south of Skokholm Island at slack water. This will give a fair tide around the Bishops and half way across Cardigan Bay if good speed is maintained. In calm weather an offing of about a mile from the Bishops will take advantage of the stronger tides inshore. Otherwise an

offing of at least four miles is advisable and passing midway between Grassholme and Skomer. It is advisable to give Skokholm an offing of at least 2 miles to avoid Wild Goose Race which forms to the west and southwest of the island.

Jeffrey's Haven beyond the Cable

Bishops Rock visible through the gap between Ynys Bery and Ramsey Island

North of the Sound, more turbulence off Trwyn Ogof Hen

The Bitches stand like a row of teeth with the tide swirling around them

Dale, a delightful anchorage inside Milford Haven but sometimes subject to swell

HARBOURS AND ANCHORAGES

Milford Haven

HW: Dover -0500

Milford Haven is easy to enter at any state of the tide and in almost any weather, though in onshore winds the entrance channel is known locally as 'the washing machine'. It can be very rough until round into the shelter of Dale or Angle Bay. It is essential to keep a good lookout for shipping movements, keeping a listening watch on VHF Ch12.

Dale

The nearest choice of berth to the haven entrance. There is a free pontoon moored in the bay during the season. This may be full but there is room to anchor. Shelter is less than perfect, a swell rolls round into the bay in winds from southerly quarters. In easterlies it can get very rough. There are few services but the pub serves food and the yacht club is very welcoming.

Angle Bay

This is an alternative anchorage if Dale is uncomfortable. There are no services and the tide runs strongly across the bay. Choose your spot according to wind direction and anchor clear of the moorings.

Milford Haven Marina

On the north side of the haven, close to the town. Access is through a lock which has entry opening times from HW-4 to HW+2¾ with free flow from HW-2¼ to HW-¼. A waiting pontoon is alongside the wall to the east of the lock entrance. There are good facilities here including showers, laundry, chandlery, repairs and engineers. Ashore there are bars and restaurants to suit a range of tastes and pockets.

PIPER'S EXPERIENCE THE BISHOPS, RAMSEY SOUND & JACK SOUND

Southward direct from Bardsey

In calm weather *Piper* and I rounded Bardsey early on the ebb, intending to face the northgoing flood in the middle of the bay where streams are weaker and to pass outside the Bishops as the tide turned once more in our favour. I was enjoying the silent but slow progress under sail and the hours passed peacefully. Unfortunately, by the time we were approaching the Bishops the tide was already turning northwards once more. We slowed to a halt and then began to go backwards. I started the motor. We moved forward for a while and then stopped again; the Bishops Rock with its light showed through the haze a mile to port as the water flowed past. For two hours the engine throbbed and the Bishops remained unmoved. At last the tide eased, *Piper* began to move over the bottom and soon St Anne's Head was in sight, and the entrance to Milford Haven.

A passage that had started peacefully ended in frustration. By anticipating the situation that a combination of wishful thinking and inertia had got me into I could have made an early decision to alter course and avoided the hours of fruitless motoring. Though Fishguard was 10 miles off my track I could have anchored there in peace and security, catching up with some much-needed sleep after the overnight passage across Cardigan Bay. Alternatively, I could have headed further offshore where the tides are much weaker than at my inshore position. Had I headed further west to pass at least four miles off the Bishops I would have made better progress and any remaining flood would have helped carry me back towards Milford Haven once I was south of Skomer Island.

Southward from Fishguard

We had a wonderful sail from Fishguard down to Strumble Head as a fresh southerly breeze drove *Piper* along in a smooth sea, sheltered by the land to windward. Rounding Strumble Head the tide was still running northwards and with *Piper* close-hauled our track took us directly towards the Bais Bank. Conditions were fairly choppy and the wind about F4 to 5. With Ramsey Sound almost dead upwind I tacked *Piper* back and forth between the North Bishops and St David's Head. She strained forward, punching through the seas and hurling spray across the foredeck. It was exhilarating sailing but our track on the GPS plotter told a depressing tale. Close-hauled and with the lee rail just awash I glanced through the hatch at the little screen. We were just retracing our track, making no windward progress at all. I tried motoring dead to windward. We made no better headway but *Piper* pitched and bucked, hurling water aft, right across the cockpit.

Back under sail I tried two more long tacks, hoping the tide would be easing in time for us to make the four miles southwards to Ramsey Sound in time for slack water. It was like trying to break through a solid wall. Try as we might there was no southward progress to be made. It was now obvious that by the time we reached Ramsey Sound the tide would be running strongly right into the teeth of the wind. Wind over tide for a first passage of Ramsey Sound was not a prospect to be relished especially as the tide through Jack Sound, turning earlier, would have already had an hour longer to run and we were still faced with a dead beat across St Bride's Bay. I headed *Piper* westwards to pass outside of the Bishops and Clerks. It was a rough ride. The seas were big and irregular and the wind continued fresh, but we had sea room to relax a little. Once the tide turned, *Piper*'s windward ability carried us swiftly south into the Bristol Channel and after an exhilarating broad reach around St Anne's Head we rolled and wallowed through the Milford Haven entrance channel. It was a great relief when we anchored at last in Dale.

Going through the Sounds

Piper has passed northwards outside the Bishops several times, each without incident. The proximity of Milford Haven as a departure point and the pleasure of remaining there make it easy to wait for suitable conditions for the trip. The wind was just north of west and light as we set out but was forecast to strengthen in blustery showers. I decided to try the inside route. I was nervous about being late for slack water and as a result I arrived too early and the tide was still running out quite strongly. I tucked *Piper* out of the run of the stream in the shelter of Skomer Island and watched the eddies swirling visibly on the surface of the water.

We waited for about twenty minutes, though the time passed quickly watching the

The South Bishop light, visible from Ramsey Sound between Midland Isle and the southern tip of Ramsey Island

seals and sea birds whilst maintaining *Piper's* position. Slack water came suddenly. The sea paused in its rush and the surface became smooth. I put the engine into gear and nosed *Piper* out towards the gap between Midland Island and the mainland. The visibility had deteriorated but Jack Sound is only short. Passing 100 metres east of the Blackstones, Tuskar Rock remained clear as we approached. No sooner was *Piper* committed to the entrance than a dense shower enveloped us. Visibility vanished to zero and the rain bounced on the sea and deck. I held our course, blind for what seemed an age, trying to sense what the current was doing to our track as I gazed through my rain-spattered specs. The plotter by the chart table was just a colourful blur. When the shower had passed we were in open water.

Clear of Jack Sound we now had St Bride's Bay to cross before passing through Ramsey Sound. Out in open water the wind had risen and I pulled down a reef in the main before cutting the engine. We covered the seven miles in good time in the lively conditions, needing just one

short tack to line us up with the sound. I started the engine and rolled up the genoa. Between Ynys Bery and Ramsey Island I caught sight of the Bishops Rock, three miles to the west. The Bitches showed clearly ahead as a row of teeth and the young flood swirled around the outer end of the reef. I aimed *Piper* at the mid-point of the gap, both hands on the tiller. The water boiled and surged and we flew through. The big circular eddy towards the island showed clearly on the surface and I felt its pull as I kept *Piper* on track for Trwyn Ogof Hen, the northernmost point of the Island. A bearing on the LB slip confirmed that we were clear of Horse Rock and I returned *Piper* to a northerly heading. Passing to the west of another patch or turbulent water I put *Piper* on a heading for St David's Head. Rounding each headland the wind came from the bow to the beam and as we cleared Strumble Head it was over the quarter. Soon we were at anchor in Fishguard, our passage through the Sounds four hours faster than my previous passage from Fishguard to Milford Haven outside of the Bishops.

Neyland Marina

On the north side of the haven, just before the Cleddau Bridge. It is 7 miles from the sea but has the advantage of not being lock controlled if you require a low water departure. Facilities include showers, laundry, chandlery and repairs. There are a restaurant and café on the quayside and a few small shops in the town.

Contacts

Dale Yacht Club ☎ 01646 636362
Milford Haven Marina ☎ 01646 696312
Neyland Marina ☎ 01646 601601
Neyland Yacht Club ☎ 01646 600627

Fishguard

HW: Dover –0400

The harbour is protected by a breakwater but in northerly winds a swell can creep inside. Entrance is straightforward and is possible in rough weather and at all states of tide. When entering or leaving beware of high-speed ferry movements. Accommodation for visiting yachts is limited. Anchoring is not permitted within the commercial harbour except SW of the ferry slip, and this area is crowded with moorings. The most popular anchorage is off the Lower Harbour, just out of the fairway. In strong southerlies the wind funnels down the harbour and better shelter can be found close under Stepper Point or Castle Point. Yachts that can take the ground can sometimes find a berth alongside the pier. The drying Lower Harbour was used as the location for the film of the Dylan Thomas poem *Under Milk Wood.* Ashore there is the Fishguard Bay Yacht Club which welcomes visiting crews.

Contacts

HM Goodwick Upper Harbour
    ☎ 01348 404453 VHF Ch 14/16
HM Lower Harbour ☎ 01348 874726
Fishguard Bay Yacht Club
    ☎ 01348 873369

Solva

A small creek tucked inside the north side of St Bride's Bay. The harbour dries but can offer complete shelter in its crowded little harbour for yachts that can take the ground. Solva is best avoided in S or SW winds. Mooring buoys are laid off the harbour or there is room to anchor behind the rock in 3m. For local advice contact the harbourmaster. There is a shop in the village and fresh water on the quay.

Contacts

Harbourmaster ☎ 01437 720153
Solva Boat Owners Association
    ☎ 0137 721488

Abercastle

51°58′N 05°07′W

This small inlet lies 4 miles SSW of Strumble Head. It can be identified by islets on either side of the inlet, approximately 40m high and 150m long. Anchor in 2m abeam of the northernmost islet. The bottom is sandy with good holding. There is good shelter from southerly quarters but the anchorage is open to the north. Supplies can be bought at the village of Trevine, 1 mile distant.

CHARTS AND PILOTS

Imray C60, C61
Admiralty: 1973, 1478, 1482, 2878
Lundy and Irish Sea Pilot David Taylor
    (Imray Laurie Norie and Wilson)

10. THE NEEDLES CHANNEL

The Isle of Wight, sitting comfortably off the middle of the English south coast, encloses one of the most famous stretches of sailing water in the world. The Solent is considered by many to be the capital of yachting. The harbours, rivers and creeks are home to thousands of yachts and boats, and yet the western entrance to this stretch of sheltered water has a reputation commanding the utmost respect from the huge number of sailors who regularly pass the famous white stacks of the Needles. To underestimate the treacherous potential of the Needles Channel is to court disaster. The tides around the Isle of Wight are strong and complex. Streams in the eastern entrance of the Solent, past Nab Tower, are relatively benign. In the western entrance, the Needles Channel and Hurst Narrows, rates attain almost 5kn at springs, quite enough to stop a small yacht in its tracks.

Approaching the Needles

In the Needles Channel the tides conspire with the shallows of the Shingles and Bridge banks to create conditions which have the capacity to surprise even the most experienced sailors.

John Goode recounts a passage, outward bound aboard a Roberts 34:
'It was a flat calm day and we had a spring ebb under us as we shot down the Needles Channel under engine.'

It had been blowing hard from the southwest. The blow had passed, the wind had died and there was a big residual swell running which met the outgoing tide at The Bridge. The result was a series of steep standing waves.
'We went with no warning from flat water to horrendous seas. The yacht climbed up them almost vertically, slipping down and submerging the cockpit and then slammed down the other side.'

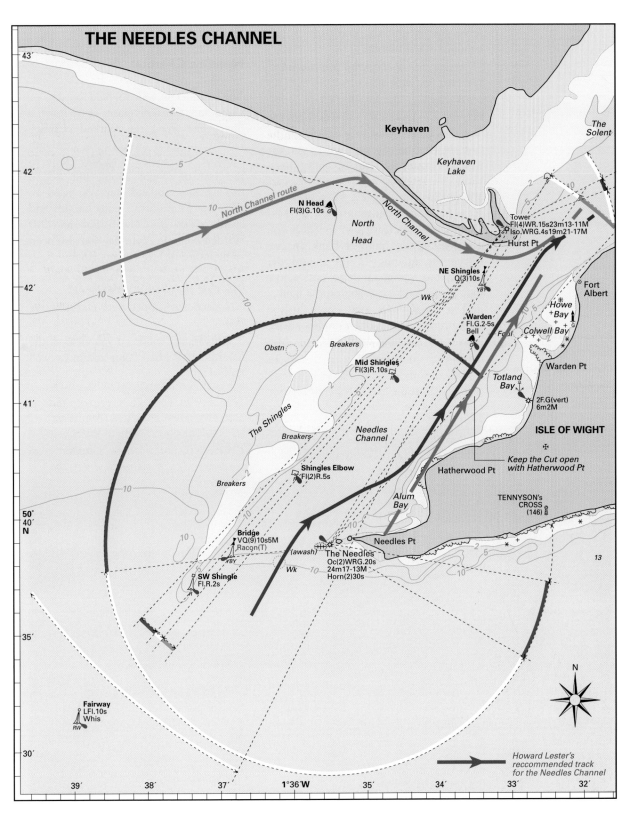

THE NEEDLES CHANNEL

Keyhaven

The Solent

Keyhaven Lake

North Channel route

North Channel

N Head
Fl(3)G.10s

North
Head

Tower
Fl(4)WR.15s23m13-11M
Iso,WRG.4s19m21-17M

Hurst Pt

NE Shingles
Q(3)10s
YBY

Wk

Fort Albert

Howe Bay

Warden
Fl.G.2·5s
Bell

Colwell Bay

Four

Obstn

Breakers

Mid Shingles
Fl(3)R.10s

Warden Pt

Totland Bay

2F.G(vert)
6m2M

The Shingles

Breakers

Needles Channel

ISLE OF WIGHT

Breakers

*Keep the Cut open
with Hatherwood Pt*

Hatherwood Pt

Shingles Elbow
Fl(2)R.5s

Breakers

50°
40′
N

Bridge
VQ(9)10s5M
Racon(T)
YBY

SW Shingle
Fl.R.2s

(awash)

The Needles
Oc(2)WRG.20s
24m17-13M
Horn(2)30s

Alum Bay

Needles Pt

TENNYSON's
CROSS
(146)

Wk

13

Fairway
LFl.10s
Whis
RW

N

FEARSOME PASSAGES

Howard Lester's
reccommended track
for the Needles Channel

John has seen his share of rough conditions, but admits:

'This was one of the scariest moments I've ever had at sea.'

Throughout the Needles Channel the tide sets strongly south and west onto the Shingles Bank. This is particularly the case on a spring ebb. Howard Lester, the RNLI's youngest cox'n, has been Yarmouth Lifeboat cox'n for two years after twelve years as crew. He reports the set as being most dangerous near the Mid Shingle buoy, increasing in speed as you get closer to the Shingles Bank. In one rescue the Atlantic 21 ILB found the current too strong for it to pull a tow rope across to the casualty on the bank.

The *Tidal Atlas* only hints at the strength of this set. John Goode's advice is to study the tidal diamonds on Chart 2035.

A yacht proceeds down the Needles Channel. Fort Albert in the distance

PILOTAGE

Needles Channel

The channel is well marked by day or night and the temptation is to take a direct line along the marked channel. Howard Lester is cox'n of the Yarmouth Lifeboat. His advice is to stay closer to the Isle of Wight shore, but before tucking into Totland Bay you need to take care to avoid the many hazards and awash rocks in Colwell Bay and off Warden Point. In Alum Bay you also need to be aware of Five Fingers Rock.

'Staying to the Isle of Wight side keep The Cut, the dry moat of the old Needles Battery, open with Hatherwood Point.'

This transit will keep you clear of the hazards off Warden Point and in Colwell Bay.

At the Bridge the fairway is less than a cable wide and at this point the seas can be at their worst. Howard's preferred option is to go nearer to the Needles, passing halfway between the Needles and the Bridge Buoy. The awash wreck at the foot of the Needles is a hazard here and has caught out more than one yacht cutting it fine during the Round the Island Race, but Howard says:

'If you can see the old coastguard station above the Needles lighthouse you are in the clear.'

A yacht proceeding down the Needles Channel between the Warden and NE Shingles E cardinal buoy

Hurst Castle

But he adds:

'It's not a very nice area anyway. When the weather's bad it's best avoided. If there is any swell or weather from the southwest the North Channel is preferable to the Needles Channel. '

North Channel

The North Channel passes north of the Shingles and North Head. In southwesterly weather conditions this is a lee shore but the proximity of the shoals to windward takes the power out of the seas. A third option is to go around the island to enter the Solent via the Nab.

Leaving the Solent cut fairly close to Hurst Point and begin making the turn in good time, before the tide pushes you too far down the Needles Channel. Do not go nearer than 200 metres to the shore at the point to avoid the turbulent water of the Trap. Once past the Trap run parallel to the beach, which is steep-to and clear of hazards. A distance of 200 metres from the shore will keep you in deep water until the North Head starboard hand buoy (Fl.3.G.10s) informs you that it is safe to lay a course for Anvil Point. Approaching the North Channel from seaward identify the North Bank buoy, which is just to the east of the village of Milford on Sea. Approaching on a northeasterly heading do not turn parallel to the beach until about 200 metres off to avoid the shallows of the North Head.

TIMING

Leaving the Solent for a passage south or west it's a relatively simple matter to time arrival at Hurst Narrows for around high water. If there's any SW or S swell the North Channel is to be preferred to avoid the rapidly building wind over tide conditions as the ebb meets the swell at the Bridge. Also, if heading for Poole or Anvil Point, the North Channel gives the most direct route.

When bound into the Solent an arrival at the Bridge the beginning of the flood would seem to be a sensible time but due to the proximity of the Bridge and Shingles Banks a vicious sea can build here as the tide turns.

Reed's Almanac warns:

'The sea state can be at its worst shortly after LW when the flood has just begun. There is then no wind-over-tide-situation but a substantial swell is raised as a result of the recently turned stream.'

Howard Lester's advice is to let the flood tide get going before approaching the Needles Channel from seaward.

In February '97 a well found charter yacht *Fairview* 2 was capsized with the loss of three of her crew when on passage into the Solent from Poole. The forecast wind was southwest Force 7 to 9. With the strong wind behind her *Fairview* 2 apparently arrived at the entrance to the Needles Channel earlier than planned, just when conditions would be at their worst. The subsequent investigation by the Marine Accident Investigation Bureau offered some useful lessons:

'. . . advice on using the Needles Channel should highlight the dangers of breaking seas in the vicinity of the SW Shingles and the Bridge bank especially in strong winds from the south round to west. The swell in such conditions tends to build up once the west-setting ebb has stopped. Around low water the seas at the seaward end of the Needles Channel can be particularly vicious.'

The indications are that because the tide was flooding, i.e. setting northeast and with the wind, the skipper decided that the Needles Channel option was a safe choice. The choice of which passage to adopt must always be the skipper's but the responsibility must be taken after very careful consideration of the dangers and,

PIPER'S EXPERIENCE NEEDLES CHANNEL

On passage down-Channel, *Piper* and I passed Nab Tower as the sun was setting. I had chosen to go through the Solent rather than south of the Isle of Wight to take advantage of the extra fair tide this would make available. My plan was to take the North Channel on rounding Hurst Point, anchoring in Studland for a sleep before continuing west. The tides were at springs but it was a new moon and the sky was like pitch. However, from the chart it looked quite simple to round Hurst Point to pass north of the NE Shingles E cardinal then pick up the N Head starboard-hand buoy 1¼ miles distant, using the sounder to guide me along the North Channel.

The entrance to Yarmouth was passed in a moment and had I entertained thoughts of stopping there I was already too late. Through Hurst Narrows the light on Hurst Castle flew by. I was nervous about getting too close to the Trap in the darkness so hesitated to make the turn. The three flashes of the NE Shingles were looming up at alarming speed. *Piper* was now firmly in the grip of the tide, travelling sideways down the Needles Channel.

The North Channel was already slipping beyond reach. I heaved the helm up to go with the flow and in the clear night picked out ahead the three red flashes of the Mid Shingles and watched astern the sectored isophase of Hurst Point. Very soon we were past the Bridge and I encountered some rougher water as the SW Shingle loomed out of the darkness. As it shrank astern I was grateful to be once more in open water and headed *Piper* for Anvil Point.

I had prepared plans for both alternatives and being in unfamiliar waters had studied the pilotage carefully, but still the strength of the tide had caught me out because of the difficulty in darkness of judging the set of the tide and its effect on my track. It was well that it was a calm night with good visibility. However, had conditions been otherwise I would have waited in the Solent for daylight.

When *Piper* and I next passed this way it was daylight with a SW3 and good visibility. This time there were no mistakes. We stayed close enough inshore off Hurst Point to make the turn. The turbulent water over the Trap showed up well and using the sounder to run parallel to the beach through the North Channel we had an uneventful trip until we reached the overfalls off Anvil Point.

if lacking in local knowledge, having taken the advice of others. In this instance the skipper, having taken the decision to proceed to sea, appeared unaware of the grave dangers associated with entering the Needles Channel in strong SSW winds, and especially in the early stages of the flood.

Despite having to sail close to a lee shore, the North Channel offers a viable and usually safer alternative to the Needles Channel when entering and leaving the Solent in adverse weather conditions even when the tide is favourable.

THE HARBOURS

Yarmouth

52°42´.4N 01°30´.05W

Begin the turn towards the entrance in good time if the tide is running, to be already stemming the flow as you pass between the East and West Fairway buoys. At night identify the lights on the end of the pier (2F.R(vert)) then try to pick out the leading lights at either end of the town quay before making a final approach. This can be difficult when there is so much light clutter nearby.

Inside the harbour berth as directed by the berthing master. Yarmouth is a very popular harbour, especially at weekends with local boats 'going foreign' from across the Solent. An illuminated sign saying 'Harbour Full' or a red flag by day at the end of the ferry jetty indicate that there is no more room inside. At these times a mooring may be available outside. Visitors' moorings are served by a water taxi.

Facilities

Showers and toilets and laundry. Limited chandlery, pubs, restaurants and a range of small shops in the town. Scrubbing berths alongside the breakwater.

Contact

Harbourmaster

☎ 01983 760321 VHF Ch 68

Lymington

50°45´.1N 01°31´.4W

Lymington is a comfortable market town with cobbled streets, close to the New Forest. Entry is straightforward and well marked once the Jack in a Basket beacon (Fl(2s)R.9m) with its basket topmark is identified. Frequent ferry traffic has right of way. Lymiongton is home to two very large marinas, Lymington Yacht Haven and Berthon's Lymington Marina. Berths are also provided for visitors at the Town Quay. If this is full the harbourmaster may be able to direct you to a mooring. The marinas are expensive even by south coast standards but the Town Quay is cheaper and closer to the town centre. Anchoring is prohibited anywhere in the river.

Facilities

The Royal Lymington Yacht Club and the Lymington Town Sailing Club both welcome visiting yacht crews. The town has a range of shops, pubs and restaurants. There is every conceivable service the sailor could require either at one of the marinas or close by in the town.

Contacts

Lymington HM ☎ 01590 672014

Lymington Marina ☎ 01590 673312
    VHF Ch 80, 37

Lymington Yacht Haven
    ☎ 01590 677071 VHF Ch 80, 37

Royal Lymington Yacht Club
    ☎ 01590 672677

CHARTS AND PILOTS

Imray C15

Admiralty 2021

Shell Channel Pilot Tom Cunliffe
    (Imray)

11. THE NORTH CHANNEL: MULL OF KINTYRE TO MULL OF GALLOWAY

At the northern end of the Irish Sea is a stretch of water sixty miles long and just twelve miles wide. Its headlands, tidal races and overfalls constitute one of the greatest challenges to a cruising yacht in the waters of the British Isles. The North Channel is gateway to the Irish Sea and is bounded to the north by the Mull of Kintyre, to the south by the Mull of Galloway and to the west by Rathlin Island and its Sound. Each has its own fearsome reputation. Harbours are few and a yacht caught out in worsening conditions may be faced with the choice of turning tail or fighting it out, at the mercy of the strong tides and the steep seas they generate in anything of an opposing wind.

THE TIDAL PICTURE

South of the Mull of Galloway the Irish Sea is an almost landlocked expanse of water a hundred miles broad. From the Isle of Man northwards the tide floods and ebbs through the North Channel, coming from and returning to the Atlantic Ocean. The tidal range is up to ten metres and as this huge mass of water comes in from the Atlantic it flows first to the east along the north coast of Ireland then turns almost at right angles to round Fair Head, some of it squeezing through Rathlin Sound before running southwards between the shores of East Antrim and Galloway. Facing Rathlin Island is the Mull of Kintyre, making this the narrowest point in its path. As the water forces its way through the narrow gap between Ireland and Scotland it also makes sudden changes of direction around the headlands, creating overfalls and races best avoided by the prudent

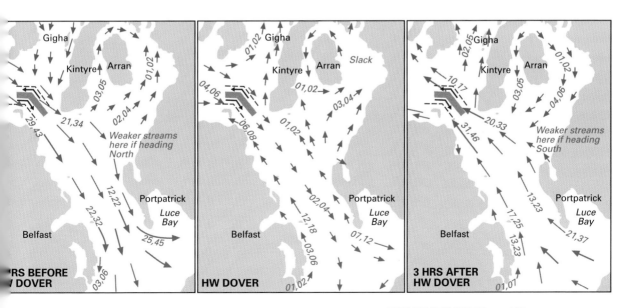

yacht skipper and tidal streams are strong throughout. To make a passage between the Irish Sea, the Firth of Clyde and the northwest of Scotland you must deal with the North Channel.

With spring rates of over 3kn in the North Channel, the only sensible option for a sailing yacht is to time a passage for a fair tide. Unfortunately, if making to or from the Hebrides and northwest coast, it is impossible to clear the difficulties before the tide turns against you. You must either break the trip to carry a fair tide all the way or put up with punching a foul tide for part of the way. Carrying a fair tide and arriving off one of the headlands near slack water there is the chance that the tide will begin to run against you before you are clear. The choices are often difficult and it is impossible to consider any of the North Channel's many challenges in isolation. A trouble-free passage through the North Channel needs careful planning.

The Mull of Kintyre lighthouse at slack water

The Mull of Kintyre

Referred to by yachtsmen simply as 'The Mull', this is the tip of the Kintyre peninsula which extends southwards from Loch Fyne towards the northeast of Ireland narrowing the gap through which the tides enter and leave the Irish Sea and the Firth of Clyde to about twelve miles. Around the Kintyre peninsula the flood runs south on the west side and north on the east side. The ebb runs north on the west side and south along the Clyde shore. Tides right across the northern entrance to the North Channel are strong, but at the Mull the turbulence generated by the restricting buttress of rock creates ferocious overfalls. Close inshore the tide runs at over 5kn at springs.

The Mull has long had a fearsome reputation among mariners but it is possible to avoid the blackest of its moods when your way lies around its

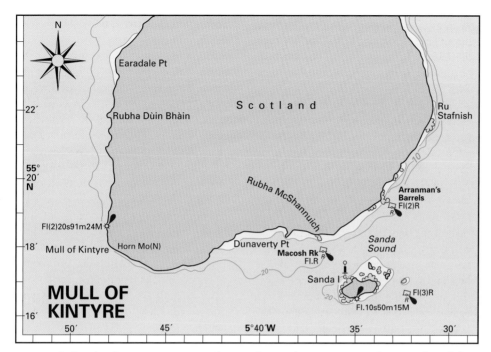

Map labels:

N

Earadale Pt

Scotland

22'

Rubha Dùin Bhàin

Ru Stafnish

55° 20' N

Rubha McShannuich

10

Arranman's Barrels
Fl(2)R

Fl(2)20s91m24M

18'   Horn Mo(N)

Mull of Kintyre

Dunaverty Pt

Macosh Rk
Fl.R

Sanda Sound

Sanda I

Fl(3)R

MULL OF KINTYRE

16'

50'   45'   5°40'W   35'   30'

Fl.10s50m15M

granite bulwark. One way is to avoid it altogether and go through the Crinan Canal. This waterway was built with the express purpose of not only reducing the sea distance from the Firth of Clyde to the islands of the west but also of providing an all-weather route from the east of the Kintyre to the west, avoiding the fearsome Mull.

Rounding the Mull westwards a natural starting point is Campbeltown but this is 17 miles from the Mull and it is over 44 miles to Gigha, the nearest secure anchorage on the west of the Kintyre Peninsula. Many skippers prefer to anchor at Sanda.

Linda Moss of the yacht *Conachair* says: *'We've been round the Mull of Kintyre on many occasions and have never had the slightest difficulty with it in either direction, always going at the recommended time of tide. The only problem is that it's a long way from Campbeltown to Gigha round the Mull. We've anchored overnight at Sanda and had the magical experience of walking over an island on which we knew there were no other people, while the tide roars round. We've always gone close inshore, inside Sanda.'*

TIDES AT THE MULL – TIME TO GO

Using the inshore route, aim to be entering Sanda Sound at about HW Dover –0100. Using the offshore route aim to be midway between Sanda and the Mull Lighthouse and about 2 miles offshore at HW Dover. Departure time from Campbeltown for both of these options in good conditions is about HW Dover –0300.

At a point 2 miles SSW of Sanda the west-going stream begins at HW Dover. Streams inshore turn more than an hour earlier. In Sanda Sound the west-going stream begins at HW Dover –0110. The east-going stream begins HW Dover +0500. This causes severe overfalls at the boundary between the two streams during the time that they are opposed. Some yachtsmen recommend staying very close in to avoid this.

Piper **sailing towards the Mull from Gigha in wind NW 4–5**

Ralph Morris of the yacht *Trilogy* says: '*We once rounded northbound with another boat, weather S/SW 2/3. We ran within almost touching distance of the cliffs and had a lovely trip. They set a 'safe distance' off and were bounced and rolled all the way.*'

Mew Island at the southern side of the entrance to Belfast Lough

Rathlin Sound

Its position, right on the angle of the Antrim coast, means that this area is going to be one of turbulence and overfalls even without the presence of Rathlin Island two miles offshore, which compresses and confuses the flow even further. Northeast of the island is the MacDonnell Race. This area of severe overfalls and eddies extends up to four miles SE from Altcarry Head on the flood. In Rathlin Sound Slough-na-more, an overfall which is dangerous at mid-tide, extends all the way from Fair Head to Rue Point. The best time to go through westwards is late in the second half of the flood, the smoothest water being found in mid-stream. The roughest water is often found between Torr Head and Fair Head. The sound is best avoided with winds above Force 5, especially if accompanied by a westerly swell.

Tides

Slack water coincides with HW Dover, the flow being westwards thereafter, and Dover+0600 when the eastward flow begins. Heading westwards aim to pass between Fair Head and Rue Point with

The western tip of Rathlin Island

Killantringan Head lighthouse 1½ miles north of Portpatrick is a good guide to finding the entrance, which can be difficult to spot until abeam

enough fair tide left to make Church Bay or Ballycastle. Making east and south, aim to be off Fair Head by Dover+0600 so that you will be clear of Torr Point before the full strength of the tide develops.

Mull of Galloway

The Rhins of Galloway is a hammerhead-shaped peninsula extending 26 miles from Corsewall Point to the Mull of Galloway at its southern tip. On the

PIPER'S EXPERIENCE RATHLIN SOUND

Portrush had been our last port of call and *Piper* was headed for the Firth of Clyde. It was a relief to have calm conditions after weeks of fighting our way up the west coast of Ireland. The aim was to carry a fair tide along the Antrim coast, passing through Rathlin Sound with an hour or so of the flood yet to run. There was little wind and the sea and sky were a deep clear blue but approaching Rathlin Island the sea swirled and heaved. *Piper*'s head was pushed this way and that as upwellings from the deep were followed by miniature whirlpools. I was early and there was still broken water in Slough na More between Rathlin and Fair Head. Whilst in Portrush I had been told of the new breakwater and approach light in Church Bay on Rathlin Island. I didn't need this haven now but I had time to kill and a look at it in good conditions may be useful for a future visit. Knowing my pilot book was not up-to-date on this change I nosed *Piper* carefully into the bay. A friendly yacht from home was just leaving: Ian and Chris taking their little Westerly Nomad *Blanche* on her annual Hebridean cruise. We waved and shouted greetings as we passed. The binoculars found the opening in the new breakwater and made out the sectored light ashore, clearly visible in daylight. For an hour I investigated ashore and then remembered my date with the tide.

Out in the Sound the swirling of the water had become less violent. We swept smoothly through Rathlin Sound and I put *Piper* on a heading for the Mull of Kintyre, clearly visible across 12 miles of smooth water. I had hoped now to be set quickly southwards on the last of the flood but I had left it too late. As I watched ahead the Mull of Kintyre started to drift southwards across *Piper*'s forestay. The ebb had begun. I decided, rather than fight the tide, to save the Firth of Clyde for another day. I now found myself in the Traffic Separation Zone and was in danger of going the wrong way up the southbound lane. With no shipping in sight we crossed at slightly less than a right angle and by evening I had joined Ian and Chris in Ardminish Bay for supper.

flood, overfalls extend several miles south of the headland. Fortunately, given the sea room at this southern end of the North Channel, the area is much easier to avoid than its cousins at the northern end.

From Luce Bay you must round the Mull of Galloway. This is best done at high water but, in westerly weather, conditions off the headland will quickly get very rough as the ebb begins to run. It is then best to go round against the last of the flood when, with wind and tide together, conditions will be much smoother. Eddies and overfalls are formed inshore at various places along

PIPER'S EXPERIENCE MULL OF GALLOWAY

I have only once sailed close to the Mull of Galloway, mainly because it lies off the direct track from the Isle of Man towards the North Channel. I had anchored overnight in a little cove at Drummore on the west side of Luce Bay, having missed the tidal window for a passage of the North Channel. Early on a fine, calm morning I rounded the Mull of Galloway, finding smooth water quite close in, just as the tide was turning. I had an idyllic passage northwards and was in Lamlash by evening.

PIPER'S EXPERIENCE MULL OF KINTYRE AND THE NORTH CHANNEL

When making the passage around the Mull from Cambelltown it is difficult to get the timing just right. On my first rounding of the Mull I was making for the Outer Hebrides and had been waiting impatiently for a break in the strong winds that were delaying a passage to Gigha. The wind was a blustery northwesterly and in timing the tide I was faced with a choice. The recommended plan is to leave about 3 hours before HW Dover and punch the tide from Campbeltown to Sanda Sound, arriving at slack water, and then have a fair tide to Gigha. This would have meant arriving at Gigha in failing light. Alternatively, I could leave Campbeltown at about 3

hours after HW Dover to take a fair tide from Campbeltown to the Mull. Rounding it on the last of the ebb I would then face a foul tide from the Mull up the west Kintyre coast. There was the possibility of the tide turning before I was far enough north of the Mull to be clear, but in the end daylight was the deciding factor. I calculated that it was worth the risk in order to get to Gigha in daylight with the evening before me and time for a meal and a pint ashore. The miles along to Sanda passed quickly. The wind was off the land and the tide helping. At Sanda I discovered just how much earlier the tide turns inshore and began to lose speed but with wind and tide together it was not too rough. Soon, though, it was down to engine power and progress was slowing rapidly. Offshore the seas looked awful, heaving and curling with crests leaping into the air. Close under the cliffs the sea

was impressive but not dangerous. At times not more that ten metres of water separated the yacht from the land. Occasionally, a huge eddy would grab the yacht's head and yank her off course but by creeping so close in I cheated the tide. Once I was past the Mull light the strength of the flow gradually eased. I wasn't in Gigha as early as I'd planned but I did get that pint.

The timing of the passage was a high-risk strategy. It was a close run thing but I got away with it. Had I been unable to round the Mull my best option would have been an early retreat to Sanda Island to wait for high water and a fair tide. I decided that night-time pilotage around the quiet shores of Gigha is much less to be feared than challenging the might of the Mull in broad daylight.

the Rhins. Smoother water is usually found about 2 miles offshore.

Tides in the North Channel
North-going begins HW Dover –0310
South-going begins HW Dover +0430
Rates attain 5kn at springs south of Black Head, 2kn at Corsewall Point.

NORTH CHANNEL STRATEGIES

Heading north on the Irish side
Having stopped over in Bangor or Carrickfergus it is an hour or so's sail out of Belfast Lough to Black Head to be in

a position to catch the northgoing ebb, making another stop at either Church Bay on Rathlin Island or Ballycastle on the north Antrim coast. It's 30 miles from here to Fair Head. Taking advantage of the lift from the tide it should be possible to maintain over 6kn over the ground. It is essential to maintain at least this speed to make harbour before the tide turns against you. Arriving off Fair Head after the turn of the tide will soon have you going backwards. It will probably be impossible to make headway into Rathlin Sound against spring rates of 6kn. The maximum rate is achieved soon after the

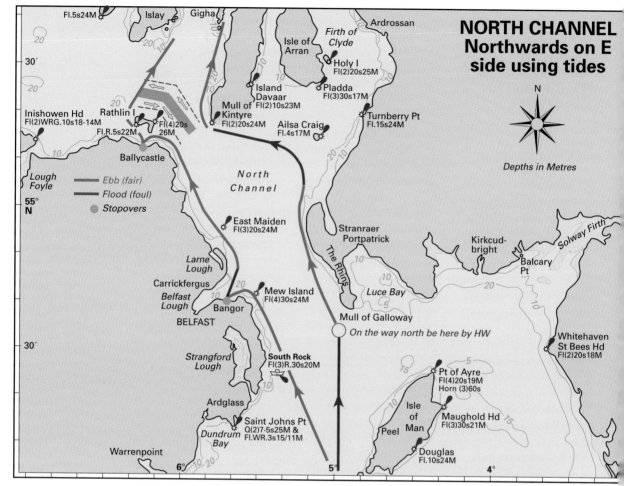

NORTH CHANNEL
Northwards on E side using tides

Fl.5s24M — Islay
Gigha
Ardrossan
Firth of Clyde
Isle of Arran
Holy I
Fl(2)20s25M
Island Davaar
Pladda
Fl(3)30s17M
Mull of Kintyre
Fl(2)20s24M
Fl(2)10s23M
Inishowen Hd
Fl(2)WRG.10s18-14M
Rathlin I
Fl.R.5s22M
Fl(4)20s 26m
Ailsa Craig
Fl.4s17M
Turnberry Pt
Fl.15s24M

N

Ballycastle

Depths in Metres

Lough Foyle

55° N

North Channel

Ebb (fair)
Flood (foul)
Stopovers

East Maiden
Fl(3)20s24M

Stranraer
Portpatrick

Kirkcud-bright

Solway Firth

Balcary Pt

Larne Lough

Carrickfergus
Belfast Lough
Bangor
BELFAST

Mew Island
Fl(4)30s24M

The Rhins

Luce Bay

Mull of Galloway
On the way north be here by HW

Whitehaven
St Bees Hd
Fl(2)20s18M

30′

Strangford Lough

South Rock
Fl(3)R.30s20M

Pt of Ayre
Fl(4)20s19M
Horn (3)60s

Ardglass

Peel
Isle of Man

Maughold Hd
Fl(3)30s21M

Saint Johns Pt
Q(2)7·5s25M &
Fl.WR.3s15/11M

Dundrum Bay

Warrenpoint

Douglas
Fl.10s24M

6°   5°   4°

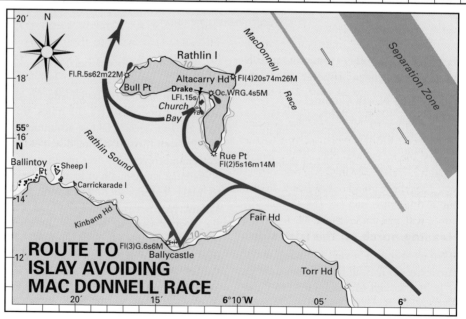

20′   N

Rathlin I

MacDonnell

Separation Zone

18′

Fl.R.5s62m22M

Altacarry Hd   Fl(4)20s74m26M

Bull Pt

Drake
LFl.15s

Oc.WRG.4s5M

Church Bay

YB

Race

55° 16′ N

Rathlin Sound

Rue Pt
Fl(2)5s16m14M

Ballintoy Pt
Sheep I

Carrickarade I

14′

Kinbane Hd

Fair Hd

12′

Fl(3)G.6s6M
Ballycastle

Torr Hd

ROUTE TO ISLAY AVOIDING MAC DONNELL RACE

20′   15′   6°10′W   05′   6°

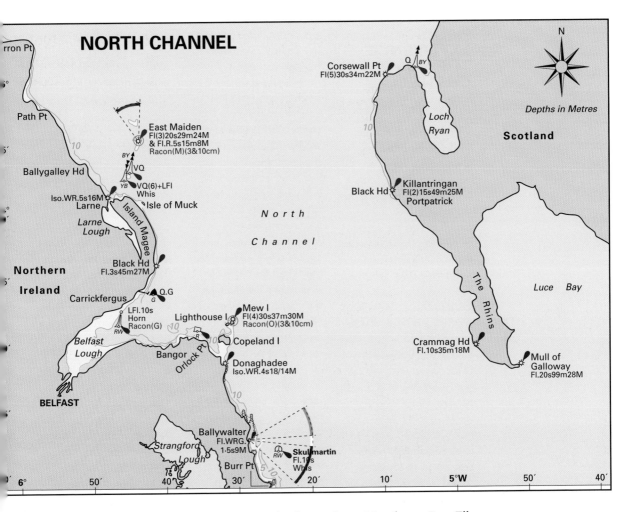

turn. If you miss the tide and are locked out of Rathlin Sound there is little choice from here but to stay at sea, making what progress you can until the tide allows you to resume good speed over the ground towards Islay, Gigha and points north.

If all goes to plan the next passage north from Rathlin will take you to the west of the island and clear of the North Channel Traffic Separation Zone. There are overfalls throughout Rathlin Sound but a departure just on the last of the flood will give time to be clear of the worst areas before the ebb gains strength. The calmest water can be found by crossing directly from Ballycastle towards Church Bay, turning for Bull Point once north of Rue Point. Once west of the

island it is about 22 miles to Port Ellen. There are no hazards in this area except for Otter Rock, 3 miles south of Texa Island, but in the presence of westerly swell or weather running against the ebb it can be rough as the strong tide passes over an uneven bottom.

North Channel Traffic Separation Zone (TSZ)

The TSZ must be either avoided, followed or crossed at right angles. From Fair Head the bearing clear of the TSZ is a direct heading for the Mull of Kintyre. This is a hard choice, but to head directly north in the inshore traffic zone east of Rathlin takes you through some of the roughest overfalls in the area of the MacDonnell Race. On the ebb this is not

PIPER'S EXPERIENCE THE NORTH CHANNEL

We left Bangor marina and headed across Belfast Lough. The wind was from the northwest and fresh, Force 4 to 5. I put one reef in the main and rolled the genoa short enough to clear the shrouds on the tacks. This would ease the work of sheeting and would make tacks quicker as Piper's head came up through the wind. The seas were short and nasty and sheets of water were thrown aft as each wave thudded into the weather bow.

Abeam of Larne Lough it was clear that despite Piper's windward ability we were not making the speed we needed to be through Rathlin Sound before the turn of the tide. I started the motor to help her through the seas. At first the inshore legs were a respite and the seas came on board less frequently. The offshore legs gave us progress northwards but were cold and miserably wet. Past Larne Lough the curve of the coastline brought the wind and sea from dead ahead of our required track and each tack was as wet as the other. My eyes were stinging, there was salt in my mouth and water was creeping down the front of my oilies. My hands were raw but only the work at the sheets kept the chill at bay. Approaching Fair Head the wind began to ease, patches of blue appeared in the leaden sky and the sunlight picked out the white of the breaking seas off Fairhead. I watched anxiously as the broken water came closer, bracing myself for the first rolling white crest. As I watched, within a few moments the water stopped piling up on itself, the white crests faded and a soft residual swell rolled uneasily in from the west. I looked up at the granite bastion of Fair Head and then across at Rathlin Island, trying to judge the distance to Ballycastle. I knew what the calm meant. The tide was turning.

The wind had continued to die down and reefs were shaken out but the tide was in control. I watched the GPS as Piper's speed over the ground dropped. It confirmed what I could already see clearly, the cliffs of Fair Head were no longer falling astern. I opened the throttle and the little Yanmar throbbed and rattled for all it was worth. For a while we edged forward. With the help from the sails we were making six knots through the water, less than half a knot over the ground. We were two miles from Ballycastle, four hours at this speed.

As I gazed up at the unmoving cliffs I considered my options. Choices were few. Astern the water had begun to curl and break in Slough na More. A retreat would mean going

a major problem, though overfalls occur to the northeast of the island. Heading south with the flood the Macdonnel Race is best avoided by following the inshore edge of the TSZ. Finding yourself east of Rathlin in bad conditions with a foul tide it may be prudent to seek the relative shelter of the Firth of Clyde, waiting until the first of the ebb to round the Mull of Kintyre. Alternatively, retreat to Larne or Belfast Lough.

Heading north on the Scots side

From the Isle of Man there is a passage of around thirty miles to time a high water arrival abeam of the Mull of Galloway. The direct course from the Calf of Man towards Portpatrick takes you well to the west of the overfalls which form off the Mull of Galloway on the flood.

The distance from The Mull of Galloway to Corsewall Point is 26 miles. It is worth remembering that in strong westerly weather Galloway will form a rocky lee shore all the way to Corsewall Point and that Portpatrick, the only harbour on this coast, may well be impossible to enter in winds of Force six and over.

through the overfalls, but where then? I hoped to gain some ground by creeping closer inshore, but going as close as I dared to the rocks made no difference. It felt like some bad dream where I was being pursued by the white breaking waves astern and couldn't get away, everything happening in slow motion. Across the sound two other yachts sat motionless off Rue Point, their bow waves telling the same story. No point trying over there, then. At long last we edged into Ballycastle Bay and *Piper* began to make discernible progress. We made harbour three and a half hours behind a yacht that had passed through Rathlin Sound less than half an hour ahead of us. The following day there was not a breath of wind. Leaving Ballycastle on the last gasp of the flood we nosed out into the Sound. Soon the tide was running westwards but we were beyond the width of the narrows and making for the open water beyond Bull Point

at the western tip of the island. Along with us was the Rival, *Tenacity*, the yacht that had preceded us into Ballycastle. Off Bull Point the water was raised in little peaks as if the bottom was being shaken. Beyond this was an area of whirlpools and eddies with some broken water. In the calm conditions it was little more than impressive. I shuddered to think what it would be like to have been there in anything of a westerly blow. The twenty miles to Islay passed uneventfully but every now and then we would cross an area of turbulence. Blisters appeared on the surface and eddies formed in the otherwise smooth sea as the tide flowed across the uneven seabed. By evening we were anchored in Lagavulin and the North Channel was behind us.

Fairhead astern, *Piper* strains towards Ballycastle

Making for the Firth of Clyde there is normally enough time to clear Corsewall Point and be in the weaker tides of the Firth before the turn when, once past Loch Ryan, the weaker flood running into the Clyde will then be in your favour. Heading farther north you have to do business with the Mull of Kintyre.

If making for the Mull you will face a foul tide as you cross the entrance to the Firth of Clyde, but your effort will be repaid by a fair tide around the Mull and a lift all the way towards Gigha and the Sound of Jura. By waiting for a fair tide at Loch Ryan or Portpatrick you will have to

wait again, either at Campbeltown or Sanda, for a tide to round the Mull.

Heading south

A southward passage of the North Channel can be less of a problem than going north. At the north end of the North Channel the tidal gates are very well defined. At the southern end the channel is broader and though the tides are strong it is within the capabilities of a yacht to make headway against them. The absence of a TSZ gives you a freer hand in choice of heading.

In light winds the overfalls to the west of Rathlin are still impressive on passage towards Islay from Ballycastle

From Islay to Ireland

Leaving from Islay for the Irish coast the TSZ has again to be negotiated. By leaving Port Ellen at about half ebb you will arrive in the area of the TSZ at around slack water. It will then be easier to cross it at right angles. Clear of the TSZ alter course to leave Rathlin Island about a mile and a half to starboard to avoid the worst of the MacDonnell Race. You can stay farther offshore if conditions demand it as this will take you into the southbound traffic lane of the TSZ which you can then follow. Passing to the east of Rathlin gives a fast ride on the tides which attain over 4½ knots at springs. Belfast Lough is a convenient stopping place but if continuing south it is best to get well offshore before Mew Island. Streams will be weaker here as the tide turns against you.

From Gigha and the Sound of Jura

From Gigha to Machrihanish, 8 miles north of the Mull, tides are relatively weak. By making a passage down the Kintyre against the ebb to arrive off the Mull at low water slack it is possible to pick up a fair flood tide across the Clyde to make Loch Ryan or Portpatrick before the tide turns. The tide inshore at the Mull turns north earlier and south later than offshore but to take a southerly route offshore you are restricted by the presence of the northbound lane of the TSZ, 2¼ miles off the Mull.

Alternatively, by arriving off the Mull before HW with enough of the flood running to carry you clear, you can punch the ebb across the Clyde to pick up the new flood off Corsewall Point. This will enable you to carry the next flood southwards right into the Irish Sea. On rounding the Mull I've found it advantageous to continue inshore through Sanda Sound before heading south, crossing the Firth of Clyde in an area of weaker streams. This will also take you clear of the worst of the overfalls SW of the Mull.

THE HARBOURS

Portpatrick

54°50´.0N 05°08´.0W

Finding the way in

Due to limited depths in the entrance, do not approach 2 hours either side of low water. The entrance is 1½ miles south of Killantringan Head Lighthouse, a 22-metre white tower at sea level. Beyond the town there is a radio mast on the hill with numerous dishes. Once the entrance has been identified, two leading marks must be picked out before making an approach. An orange stripe on the sea-wall must be aligned with another orange stripe on the gable end of a house on the left of the street running up from the harbour. Turn to enter the inner harbour as soon as it opens to port. Visiting yachts berth alongside the wall on the shoreward side of the inner harbour or as directed by the harbourmaster. There are plans for a pontoon to expand the capacity of the harbour, which is very popular at weekends with Irish sailors. Either side of the entrance are the ruins of old breakwaters. It can be impossible

to enter Portpatrick in strong onshore winds, when the entrance shows up as a narrow gap in a line of breaking surf.

Facilities

There is a range of shops in the town and friendly pubs, most of which serve excellent food.

A shower and toilet block is situated on the quay at the northwest corner of the harbour. The harbourmaster's office is close by. Diesel is available.

Portpatrick from above the inner harbour

Portpatrick. Visiting yachts berth in the inner harbour along the shoreward quay

Tides
Dover +0037
MHWS 3.8m MLWS 0.3m

Ballycastle
55°12´.7N 06°15´.0W

Tucked into the centre of Ballycastle Bay to the west of Fairhead, this little town has recently expanded harbour facilities, pontoon berths with water and power alongside. Entrance is straightforward, turning to port once through the new breakwaters, but approaching from Fair Head stay at least two cables offshore until abeam of the entrance to avoid rocks and ground swell inshore.

Facilities
Showers and toilets by harbourmaster's office 50 metres from the slip. Power and water alongside.

This popular little holiday town has shops, pubs, banks and a post office. There is an excellent fishmongers close to the harbour.

Tides
Tides are rather irregular.
HW *Springs* Dover –0445
HW *Neaps* Dover –0200

Church Bay
55°17´.4N 06°12´.5W

Church Bay has a new breakwater, providing better shelter in the inner harbour and creating more sheltered anchoring space. On entering the bay make for the church until the new breakwater opens. A sectored light is established at the left end of the long white building ashore. A shallow patch (wreck 0.8m) in the middle of the bay is marked with a S cardinal buoy. The ferry uses the concrete jetty but a berth can usually be found alongside, inside the old breakwater.

Limited facilities, but there is a pub and a post office.

Tides as Ballycastle.

Loch Ryan
54°58´.5N 05°03´.0W

Stranraer, a busy ferry port for crossings to Ireland, lies at the head of Loch Ryan. There is some accommodation for yachts in the harbour alongside the west pier. For a quieter night anchorage may be had at the Wig on the west side of the loch, though in northerly winds a swell does get around the Spit. In strong south to

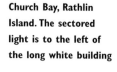

Church Bay, Rathlin Island. The sectored light is to the left of the long white building

southwest winds Stranraer harbour would be more comfortable.

Facilities

At the Wig: the sailing club allows visiting yacht crews to use their showers when the clubhouse is open.

At Stranraer harbour: shops, post office, bank, Calor Gas. Petrol and diesel at the garage.

Tides

NW stream begins Dover +0115, turning SE after 5½ hrs
Constant Dover +0055
MHWS 3.0m MLWS 0.2m

Sanda Island

55°17´.0N 05°35´.0W

The anchorage is on the north side of the island. There is a drying reef in the middle of the bay. Enter from due north, keeping over towards the pier. A green metal beacon marks the reef on the west side of the bay. Subject to swell.

Tides Dover +0035
MHWS 2.4m MLWS 0.4m

Campbeltown

55°25´.0N 05°35´.0W

Campbeltown is a moderate-sized town tucked behind Island Davaar at the head of Campbeltown Loch. Entry is easy at all states of tide and in any weather. The harbour is at the head of the loch and shelter is excellent.

Facilities

Visitors' pontoons, diesel, Calor Gas, Camping Gaz, shops, post office.

Tides

Constant Dover +0125
MHWS 3.4m MLWS 0.3m

Drummore

54°41´.5N 4°51´.8W

Scotland's southernmost village has a drying harbour where visitors may lie alongside the pier. Entry limited to 2½ hours either side of HW. The harbour is unlit and should not be approached at night. Anchorage in 3m off the harbour entrance.

Tide Dover +0015

The church is a conspicuous mark in Church Bay, Rathlin Island

12. ORFORD BAR

The lovely Norman town of Orford is separated from the North Sea by a long arm of shingle. The river, coming so close to the sea at Aldeburgh, turns away at the last moment to wind for another nine miles passing inland of Orford Ness, emerging at last almost reluctantly at Orford Haven as if unwilling to be blended with the cold waters of the North Sea. The shingle strip of Orford Ness was formed by the power of the waves and the drift of shingle down the Suffolk coast. Today the Ness is a nature reserve but the area has a warlike history. It was used in the First World War as a test range for bombing and aircraft guns. The first radar was developed here during the Second World War and during the Cold War the Ness was used in the development of nuclear weapons. Predating these modern remnants, the Martello Towers that stand on this coast were built in the early 19th century as a defence against the forces of Napoleon.

For centuries this coast has been in the front line of invasions from the Romans, the Danes and, from the beginning of time, the sea. On Admiralty charts from 1812 the entrance is shown as being 1.5 miles further south, between the two Martello towers. The entrance is still changing under the eternal onslaught of wind and tides. Movement between

The bungalow above the beach is the mark to guide the passage across the Bar

The Oxley port hand buoy. Near here was the shallowest part of the Bar when Piper last visited. Beyond to the left is one of the Martello towers

Very close to the beach in front of the bungalow

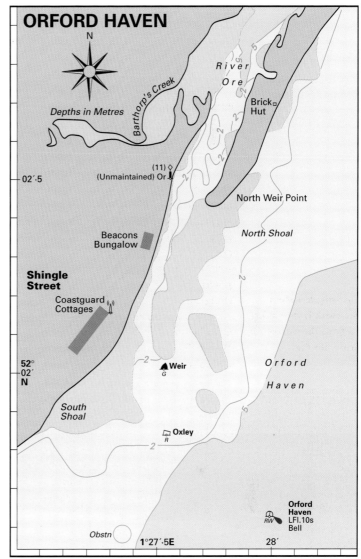

ORFORD HAVEN

N

Depths in Metres

Barthorp's Creek

River Ore

Brick Hut

(11)
(Unmaintained) Or

North Weir Point

Beacons Bungalow

North Shoal

Shingle Street

Coastguard Cottages

Weir
G

Orford Haven

South Shoal

Oxley
R

Obstn

Orford Haven
RW LFl.10s
Bell

52° 02'.5

52° 02' N

1°27'.5E

28'

the peaceful stretches of the river and the powerful forces of the open sea is only possible by passing through this battle zone.

The key to a safe passage is up-to-date information. One bad storm can completely reshape the banks and channels. **Whatever detailed description is reproduced here, it is for the interest of the reader only and will be out of date by the time it reaches the bookshelves.** A guide to Orford Haven is published each spring and is available from Small Craft Deliveries in Woodbridge ☎ 01394 382600 or www.woodbridgecruisingclub.co.uk

Piper and I visited in 1998 and headed for the roof of the bungalow above the shingle beach on a course almost due west from the Haven Buoy. By 2004 the approach course was nearer north. Ian

The sea breaks on the shingle

Making for seaward against the flood, the orange triangular beacon is to the right of the picture

A quiet anchorage in the river

Coventry of Aldeburgh Yacht Club reported the Orford Haven buoy as being off station at the time of writing. His advice was as follows:

'At the moment, find the red Oxley buoy and head 340° from this, leaving the Weir buoy about 50 metres to starboard. The trick is to stay on a line between the Oxley buoy and the bungalow which just shows above the beach. It's easier to identify this if you first look for the row of coastguard cottages just to the south. Then hug the beach until you pass the triangular beacon. Of course, all this will have changed with the next gale.'

A revised chart of the entrance is issued each year by Aldeburgh YC. This and the Orford Haven guidelines prepared by the Alde and Ore Association are available by post from the yacht club.

Tides
Orford Haven Bar
Walton on the Naze HW -0028
LW -0037
Range *Springs* 2.8m *Neaps* 1.6m

The Norman Keep at Orford is visible for many miles across the low landscape

On Orford Ness the pagodas were used in the development of Britain's nuclear weapons. The structure is designed to minimise the effects of an accidental explosion during tests on the detonators for atom bombs. The Ness was used as a base for development of radar in the Second World War and in the First World War for testing aircraft guns

After the tension of the Bar, crossing the quiet reaches of the Ore is a welcome contrast

The moorings off Orford Quay. There are some visitors' moorings available by arrangement with the harbourmaster

Orford Quay. The harbourmaster's office is in the building to the right

THE HARBOURS

Orford

The little town of Orford is dominated by its Norman keep. Small rustic brick cottages crowd the narrow streets and grander houses stand coyly screened in garden walls and shrubbery. At the quay a small ferry shuttles between the town and the Ness and the activity of the yacht club give the place a lively air.

A short walk up from the river, the Jolly Sailor fits perfectly into its surroundings. Behind its low door the pub offers liquid refreshment to thirsty mariners, and excellent seafood. Many of the timbers in its construction came from

PIPER'S EXPERIENCE ORFORD BAR

Piper was in Southwold on her way round Britain. The morning had seen only light breezes but as the tide turned it seemed to freshen. It had risen to Force 4 by the time I set off, and being from the southeast was against the tide. I bashed on anyway, keen to meet up with a new autopilot that friends in Orford had kindly taken delivery of for me. The sea was rough and breaking across the foredeck and the cockpit was ankle deep for much of the time, the water cold and brown. From Aldeburgh I cut inshore of the Aldeburgh Ridge and was protected from the worst of the sea for a time. Then I hit the overfalls just south of the Orfordness lighthouse. I bounced about a bit here but didn't take any on board as the seas were not as steep and sharp. At last I cleared the rough water as I approached the Haven buoy. I swung *Piper* around the buoy, picking out the Martello tower on the shore.

My instructions were to head towards the beach until the channel inside the shingle banks opened to starboard. The wall of orange shingle rose steeply ahead, appearing almost vertical. Above it the roof of a bungalow just showed. I felt as if I was on the beach before I could see up

the narrow entrance behind the shingle banks. Turning into the channel the sea sighed and hissed on the semi-submerged islets. Water broke over the shallows and remnant wavelets spread into the smoother waters of the channel. It took complete faith in the instructions to keep going when the channel was hidden behind the shingle islets with white foam all around them. At last there was dry ground between *Piper* and the North Sea. Once inside, the way opens and the river is amazingly calm and peaceful, gliding along between low banks topped with grass. In the distance I could see the Norman keep of Orford Castle and the parish church. To seaward, very close, was the Orfordness lighthouse which I had passed an hour or so ago in very contrasting conditions.

I anchored just inside the northern arm of the river near Cuckolds Point, Havergate Island. As the sun disappeared I sat in the cockpit and listened to the birds in the reeds, in the air and on the water. When darkness was fully come the sky was a dome studded with

bright stars and painted across with the pale light of the Milky Way with shooting stars so sudden and so bright that I wondered had I really seen them. Across the war-scarred Orford Ness the North Sea growled on the shingle.

On the morning of my departure I awoke in time for the shipping forecast and got ready for sea. The morning was calm and mild with a watery light across the anchorage. I chugged quietly down the river punching the strengthening flood. With three hours remaining of a rising tide the shingle banks, almost covered on our entrance, showed clear to seaward and being visible seemed less threatening. I wound the engine up to full throttle to finally break out of the river across the bar, turning to seaward under the looming presence of the beach. Once clear of the shallows, I wasn't quite sure where the shallows ended and the sea began in these sand-bar ridden waters. I put *Piper* on a heading for the Sunk lightship, dodging big ships and fast ferries in and out of Harwich as we set sail across the Thames Estuary.

Orfordness lighthouse seen from seaward

ships wrecked along this coast. Whilst so many streets and houses along the coast have vanished into the sea due to erosion, the Jolly Sailor finds itself further inland, having once stood on the quayside.

Facilities

In the town there are a post office and shops for provisions, including a butcher and grocer.

Berthing

There are two visitors' buoys off the quay. Lying alongside the quay is permitted only for short periods to drop off or pick up so long as the ferry landing is not obstructed. There are several completely sheltered anchorages in the river.

Contact

Town Trust harbour office
☎ 01394 459950 VHF Ch 8 *Chantry*

Aldeburgh

Just below the village of Aldeburgh, Slaughden is now mostly beneath the North Sea. At Aldeburgh the yacht club welcomes visitors, who are offered use of their showers and toilets. The river is navigable to most cruising yachts to Barber's Point, just above the town. Visitors' moorings are available. Application should be made at Upson's Yard at Slaughden Quay.

Contact

Upson's Yard ☎ 01728 453047

CHARTS AND PILOTS

Imray C28, 2000 series – 2000.2
East Coast Pilot Colin Jarman, Garth Cooper and Dick Holness (Imray)

Orford Quay

13. PORTLAND RACE

The limestone arrowhead of Portland is one of the most dramatic features of the English Channel coastline. Often referred to as the 'Isle of Portland', it is really a peninsula, joined to the mainland by Chesil Beach, a pebble strand stretching several miles to the west. Portland is referred to in Thomas Hardy's novels as the 'Isle of Slingers'. The story goes that in bygone days its inhabitants would discourage visitors from the mainland, using the pebbles of Chesil beach as a ready source of ammunition.

From east or west the Portland appears as a wedge of rock, tapering from the high point at the Verne down to The Bill, the southernmost tip of the island, but it is not the rock that is the major hazard. Looking out to sea from The Bill an area of water shows white and broken even in calm weather. Waves leap and tumble in all directions, breaking and flinging spray high into the air as if the sea is being shaken. This is the Portland Race. Portland Race truly has a fearsome reputation. Many of the visitors picnicking on The Bill or enjoying a cream tea at the Lobster Pot Café have come just to see The Race.

Portland Race is the most dangerous extended area of broken water in the English Channel. Quite substantial vessels drawn into it have been known to disappear without trace.

Tom Cunliffe *The Shell Channel Pilot*
For yachts on passage in the English Channel, whether heading east or west, getting around this obstacle whilst also avoiding The Race and the Shambles Bank, remains one of the major challenges to be faced by a yacht skipper.

THE TIDAL PICTURE

The tide flows strongly east and west in the English Channel. Portland extends five miles southwards from the Dorset coastline, interrupting this flow. During all but two hours of each tide there is a strong flow southwards along both sides of Portland. Where these two currents meet each other and run into the main tide of the Channel the sea bed is uneven. A shelf of rock extends out from the Bill, forcing water to well up from the bottom. It is difficult to imagine a richer recipe for chaos. The resulting disturbance gives us what is possibly one of the most dangerous stretches of water in the British Isles and certainly in the Channel: the Portland Race.

Portland lighthouse with its distinctive red band

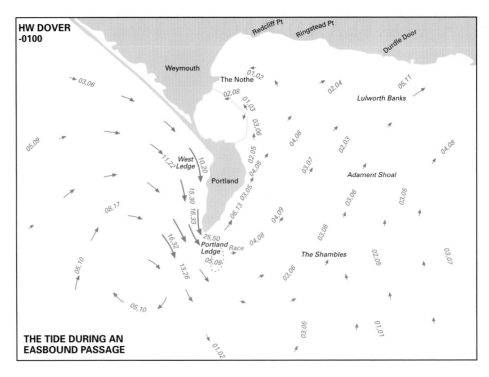

THE TIDE DURING AN
EASBOUND PASSAGE

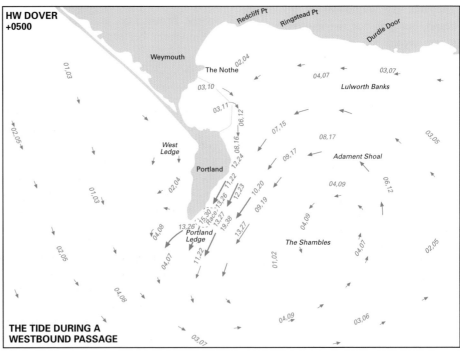

THE TIDE DURING A
WESTBOUND PASSAGE

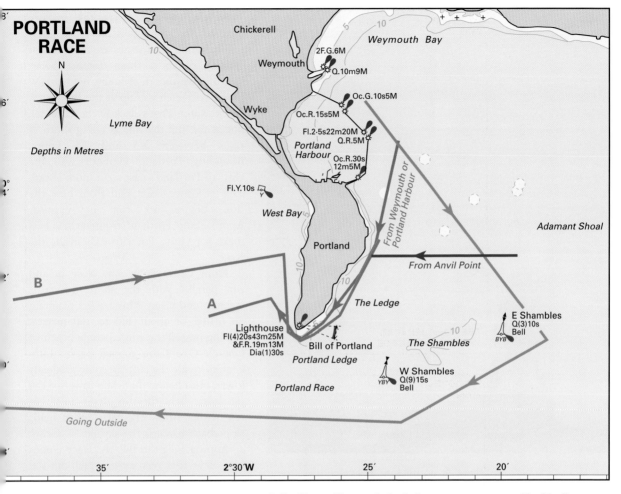

PORTLAND RACE

N

Depths in Metres

Lyme Bay

Chickerell

Weymouth

Wyke

Weymouth Bay

2F.G.6M
Q.10m9M

Oc.G.10s5M

Oc.R.15s5M

Fl.2·5s22m20M
Q.R.5M

Portland Harbour

Oc.R.30s 12m5M

Fl.Y.10s

West Bay

Portland

From Weymouth or Portland Harbour

From Anvil Point

Adamant Shoal

B

A

The Ledge

Lighthouse
Fl(4)20s43m25M
&F.R.19m13M
Dia(1)30s

Bill of Portland

Portland Ledge

The Shambles

The Shambles

E Shambles
Q(3)10s
Bell
BYB

W Shambles
Q(9)15s
Bell
YBV

Portland Race

Going Outside

35′   2°30′W   25′   20′

TIMING AND PILOTAGE

Despite all this, with care and prudent timing it is possible to get around Portland without getting badly beaten up or sunk. The options are between inshore and offshore passages. Calling at Weymouth, the inshore passage saves considerable distance compared to the outside route. Going via the offshore route you need to pass at least three or up to five miles south of the Bill. This is a long way round if leaving from or going to Weymouth, and in bad weather you would be wise to consider staying in the fleshpots until the conditions are more favourable for the long crossing of Lyme Bay. Sailing directly up or down Channel

A. If calling at Weymouth the inshore passage saves considerable distance compared to the outside route. If continuing up or down Channel there is nothing to be gained by going inside

The inshore passage is dangerous in rough conditions, especially in the presence of a SW swell. Leaving an offing of 3 miles from Portland Bill will take a yacht clear of the Shambles Bank but in rough weather a clearance of five or more miles may be needed

B. From Lyme Bay make for Blacknor Point to avoid being swept into the Race by the strong southerly set as you approach the Bill. From the east, close the Portland shore at Grove Point to pass inside the Race

There are rocks awash at high water close inshore between Pulpit Rock and the white stone beacon

If you arrive early from the west it is best to await a fair tide in West Bay except in strong south westerlies when it would be better in any case to go outside the Race

Arriving from the west you need to allow for the strong southerly stream that you will encounter as you approach the Bill. This can be seen clearly in the Admiralty Tidal Atlas and in the tidal charts opposite

Being so close inshore, most yachts opt to motor-sail around the Bill

Making westward via the inshore passage the timing is easy as good harbours and anchorages are plentiful for starting points a short distance away. Leaving Weymouth 2 hours before HW Dover will fetch you up at the Bill just at 'slack' water. That's slack in the Channel, but at the Bill the tide is going south at rates between 2.5 and 4.6 knots. Rounding Portland Harbour wall the cliffs of Portland's east coast loom ahead. This is Grove Point and from here the tide begins to run in earnest. Approaching Portland from farther east make for Grove Point to pass inside the Race.

From Grove Point stay close in and run parallel with the shore, which is steep-to and clean. Most yachts maintain an offing of about 100 to 150 metres. Having passed the white pebble beach of Church Ope Cove topped by its 13th-century castle the cliffs become gradually lower, until below the white tower of the old lower light they are down to about ten metres. Above the cliffs, green fields slope back towards the skyline.

Approaching the Bill, the Race comes into view. It is very easy to pick out the strip of smooth water between the Race and the rocks, like a tarmac road through rugged country, narrowing down towards Pulpit Rock at the very tip of Portland. Ashore, wooden beach huts cluster on the grass and the barber's pole red and white of Portland lighthouse towers against the sky. At its foot, closer to the sea is a white pyramid beacon. From this point the cliffs turn northwards and Pulpit Rock comes into view, beyond it the open waters of Lyme Bay.

One hazard to watch out for is pot markers. These are often small and when the tide is running hard can be pulled beneath the surface by the flow. This is especially dangerous as most yachts will round the Bill under engine. Between the white beacon and Pulpit Rock there are rocks awash extending from the shore.

there is nothing to be gained by going inside.

The inshore passage is dangerous in rough conditions, in the presence of a SW swell or in strong wind over tide conditions, especially at springs. But when conditions are right the inshore passage holds no terrors for a competent yacht skipper and will give you a wonderful lift on your way, as well as saving several miles of sailing in the 'wrong' direction.

Peter Jackson of Weymouth Sailing Club has been round the inshore passage 20 to 30 times and says:

'I've never had a problem with it. At the right time and in the right conditions it's fine. I think St Alban's Head is much worse.'

Portland Bill from Lyme Bay, with Pulpit Rock to right

Approaching the Bill: the derrick (used to lift fishing boats up the cliff), the lighthouse and the beacon

Once clear of Pulpit Rock West Cliff opens. Against the skyline stand the rectangular buildings of what was once the Admiralty Underwater Weapons Establishment. You are once again in open water but here you will encounter the south-going flow from the west side of Portland. To avoid being swept by this back into the Race, head northwest into Lyme Bay for a mile or so before laying a direct course for Start or Brixham.

Coming from the west aim to be off the Bill at Dover +0500. With this timing you will catch the narrow window of fair tide down the east side of Portland.

Most of the problems occur when eastbound, partly because of the difficulty of timing your arrival after a passage from the other side of Lyme Bay. To avoid being drawn into the Race when arriving from the west make initially for Blacknor Battery, from seaward the highest point of West Cliff. If you arrive early, local advice is to tuck into the west side of Portland and wait for the tide to turn. Unfortunately, there is nowhere here that a yacht could safely anchor, but observing a yacht's drift on the tide is an excellent way of judging the right moment to go.

Make your final approach to the Bill from the northeast, making for a point about 100 metres off Pulpit Rock, then run parallel with the cliffs round to Grove Point.

Pulpit Rock, identifiable even through fog as *Piper* feels her way around the Bill

PIPER'S EXPERIENCE PORTLAND RACE

To make the inshore passage of the Bill had been an ambition of mine since early childhood. During a family picnic at the Bill I was entranced by the sight of two yachts which hove into view from the direction of Weymouth, seeming to brush the rocks before vanishing slowly into the haze across Lyme Bay. I remember thinking, 'One day I'm going to do that.'

It was over forty years later that *Piper* and I left Weymouth 2 hours before high water Dover, the advice of my uncle George, once a local fisherman, ringing in my ears in his strong Dorset accent:

'Stay close enough to the rocks so you can spit on her and don't look behind. When you get around Pulpit Rock head into Lyme Bay for a mile or so or she'll have you back into the Race.'

From Grove Point I got about 100 metres offshore and watched the features of the Portland shoreline sweep swiftly by. As we approached the Bill I did ignore George's advice not to look behind. Not far away the sea was in turmoil, waves leaping and breaking in all directions. *Piper* was in a narrow strip of smooth water. Offshore from us another yacht was on a parallel course, barely a hundred metres away and having a very rough time of it. Following Uncle George's advice we had a tense but straightforward passage and soon Portland was astern and *Piper* was bounding away across Lyme Bay, a longstanding promise fulfilled.

Our latest rounding of the Bill, again from the east, was less simple. We left Portland harbour on a fine morning,

looking forward to a pleasant passage down Channel. Around Grove Point the tide's firm embrace was drawing us towards the Bill when suddenly we ran into a solid wall of fog. The tide was only a day or so off springs and there was no question of turning back. Whether we faced forwards or backwards we were going around the Bill.

There was a slight swell running up from the southwest which crashed onto the rocks to starboard. Ironically, this made navigation easier. Through the gloom I could just make out the white of the surf as it burst ashore.

Remembering my previous passage I knew I could stay very close in and proceeded by estimating distance off by the sound of the surf. In a brief clearance I dimly made out the derrick used to lift boats up the cliffs. Ahead, I scanned the water for pot markers.

I could hear the foghorn at the Bill light, getting nearer with every blast. Its blaring note was very loud abeam for a few moments then faded again. I was off the lighthouse. I watched the steering compass and continued to follow the whiteness and sound of the surf on the rocks. Pulpit Rock appeared through the mist, square and unmistakable. Running parallel to the cliffs our heading gradually changed. As the heading became almost northerly I knew I was now in Lyme Bay on the west side of Portland. I headed *Piper* northwest and continued on this course for a couple of miles before finally putting *Piper* on a direct bearing for Start Point, 20 miles away across open water.

Pulpit Rock

'Watch for the south-going set near the Bill. Crossing Lyme Bay make for a point at least three miles north of the Bill. It is too easy to get within three miles of the Bill and be met by five knots of south-going tide which will throw you straight into the Race.'

Mike Jury of Weymouth SC

IF IT GOES WRONG

Yachts do get drawn into the Race, either by bad timing, inaccurate navigation or just plain bad luck. Local fisherman Alan Smith fishes for bass off the Bill. His advice for anyone unfortunate enough is:

'Don't try to fight it. Drop your sails and go with it. It will be a very unpleasant experience but the Race won't take long to spit you out at the other end.'

Weymouth lifeboat is regularly called to small vessels caught up in the Race.

THE HARBOURS

Weymouth

50°36´.6N 02°26´.5W

Weymouth is the quintessential English seaside town. Developed as a resort by the Victorians, it remains a popular family holiday destination. The wide, gently shelving beach of fine golden sand is perfect for bathing and the seafront has the traditional mix of guest houses, amusements and shops, a wide promenade and the ornate Victoria Clock.

The harbour is in the river Wey, protected at its entrance by a breakwater and the Nothe, on which stands the Nothe Fort. Mandatory IPTS control entry. At night leading lights on the Nothe give an entry bearing of 240°. The north pier has fixed green lights (2F.G(vert)9/7m6M) and the south pier has a flashing white light (Q.10m9M). To starboard on entry is the ferry quay which serves a high-speed service to the Channel Isles. Beyond this is the Harbour

Weymouth Harbour, looking from the Cove towards the Nothe

Office and berths for larger visiting yachts. To port are resident boat moorings and a fuelling berth, close to which is Weymouth Yacht Club. There are berths in the cove for smaller visiting craft. On both sides of the harbour are several good pubs. The Town Bridge lifts to give access to the marina which has serviced pontoon berths.

Facilities

Toilets and showers in the harbour office. Weymouth has growing popularity as a yachting centre and has chandlery, engineers, repairs and sailmakers as well as all the shops and services of a medium sized town. Fuel is available alongside close to Weymouth Yacht Club but there have been problems with water in the diesel.

IPTS No lights showing – entrance clear, enter or leave with caution.

2 reds over 1 green – entry and departure prohibited. Entrance obstructed.

Contact

Harbourmaster ☎ 01305 206426
   VHF Ch 12
Marina ☎ 01305 767576

Portland

50°35′.8N 02°26′.0W

Portland harbour was once a major naval base and is an excellent ship harbour. For a yacht however, the very size of the harbour can be a problem as there is sufficient fetch to allow an uncomfortable sea to develop in strong winds. Yachts should enter by the North Ship Channel, first calling Portland Harbour on Ch 74. There are moorings laid in the season near Castle Cove Sailing Club. Visitors' moorings may be available through the sailing club or through the Royal Dorset YC. Or anchor near the New Channel beacon, clear of the moorings.

Facilities

There are few facilities for visiting yachts. Fresh water from the tap in the Sailing Club dinghy park.

Contacts

Harbourmaster ☎ 01305 824044
   VHF Ch 74
Castle Cove YC ☎ 01305 783708
Royal Dorset Yacht Club
   ☎ 01305 786258

Portland and harbour viewed from the northwest

14. RAZ DE SEIN

The Pointe du Raz stands between the Baie de Douarnenez and the Baie d'Audierne. For a yacht sailing from Britain, all coasts have up to this point faced the north and the weather has been that of the English Channel. Once past the Pointe du Raz there is a noticeable change. Suddenly you are in the south, sensing that you have found what you left England in search of. The winds feel warmer and the tides are less ferocious than those you have passed through to get to this point. From the Baie de Douarnenez only one obstacle stands in your way, the Raz de Sein.

The Raz is a vicious tide race running off the Pointe du Raz, a popular subject for poster-sized prints of rough seas with huge waves breaking across the La Vieille lighthouse. There is a local saying about the Raz de Sein:

'No-one passes here without fear or sorrow.'

Offshore from the Pointe du Raz lies the Ile de Sein, a small rocky island which forms the inshore end of Le Chaussée de Sein, a chain of reefs and rocks extending for 13 miles westwards, out into the Atlantic. Beyond this lies open ocean with the nearest land over three thousand miles away, and the mature ocean swells crash with tremendous force against the granite shores of Brittany. That swell, in combination with the tides and local weather can make conditions very rough in the area of the Raz.

The tides run generally north and south along this coast and are compressed by the arrowhead of the Pointe du Raz peninsula, jutting westwards into its flow. The tide is further thwarted in its progress by the Chaussée de Sein and it is forced to rush

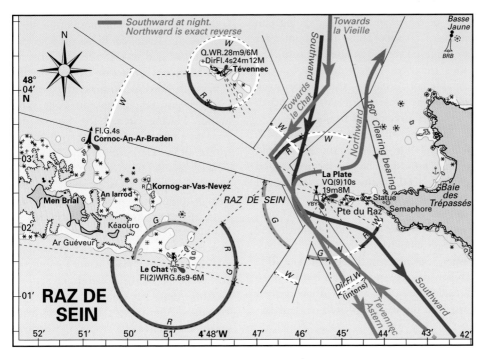

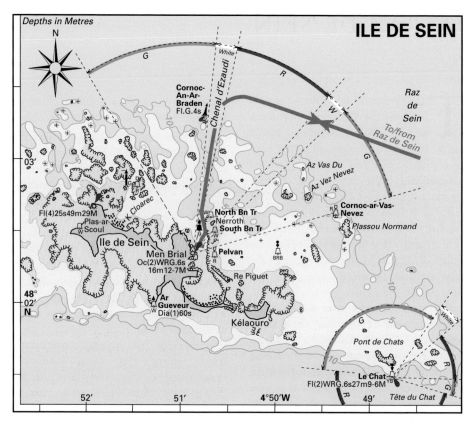

Depths in Metres
N

ILE DE SEIN

Cornoc-
An-Ar-
Braden
Fl.G.4s

Chenal d'Ezaudi

White

G

R

W

Raz
de
Sein

To/from
Raz de Sein

G

Az Vas Du

Az Vez Nevez

Fl(4)25s49m29M

K Cloarec

Plas-ar-
Scoul

Ile de Sein

Men Brial
Oc(2)WRG.6s
16m12-7M

North Bn Tr
Nerroth
South Bn Tr

Pelvan

Re Piguet

BRB

Cornoc-ar-Vas-
Nevez

Plassou Normand

03'

48°
02'
N

Ar
Gueveur
Dia(1)60s

Kélaouro

Pont de Chats

Le Chat
Fl(2)WRG.6s27m9-6M

G

White

R

G

Tête du Chat

52'   51'   4°50'W   49'

through a gap less than two miles in width. The north-going flood attains rates of 6.5kn and the south-going ebb attains 5.5 knots. These maximum rates are achieved very soon after the turn. The tides run over a very uneven bottom, capable of creating turbulence even without the presence of wind and ocean swell. It is a recipe for trouble.

At neaps in calm weather, or with wind and tide together, the Raz should present little difficulty to the well found yacht. Indeed, in the right conditions it can be smoother in the passage between La Plate and the Ile de Sein than outside, but at springs or with wind against tide a passage should only be made at slack water. Strong winds against the tide create dangerous overfalls with steep breaking seas which are often at their worst on the windward side of the Raz.

THE PASSAGE OF THE RAZ

Southbound yachts will most often stop over in the Rade de Brest or Baie de Douarnenez and so will often be arriving from Morgat, Camaret or Douarnenez. It is possible, however, to make the passage direct from the Chenal du Four (see above). Having cleared the Chenal du Four on a fair tide it is less than 20 miles to the Raz. The tide in the Iroise is weaker than in the passages at either end. Maximum spring rates are typically less than 1 kn and across rather than against a yacht's track between Pointe de St Mathieu and the Raz. It is quite possible, therefore, for a yacht to arrive at the Raz too early. To await slack water temporary anchorage in southerly winds or settled weather may be found in Baie des Trépassés. Alternatively, Les Iles de Sein makes an interesting stopover, worth a visit for its own sake.

For a northbound yacht a stopover at Audierne makes a final leg of 10 miles towards the Raz. If heading for a harbour in the Iroise then a passage of the Raz at low-water slack will give a fair tide for the onward leg.

In good weather the anchorage in Anse de Sainte Evette allows a departure at any time, but in moderate to fresh southerlies this bay can be very uncomfortable. A more secure refuge can be found up the river in Audierne harbour. However, limitations on entry and exit from Audierne mean that a yacht will have to be away as soon as possible on the second half of the flood to be in time to pass through the Raz close to high-water slack.

There are few inshore hazards from Audierne to the Raz, so by staying within about half a mile offshore the main strength of the foul tide can be avoided. However, even at springs this will be under a knot. For a direct passage to the Chenal du Four a transit of the Raz at high-water slack will give time for arrival at Pointe de Saint Mathieu for the next north-going flood. As with the southward trip, the foul tide across the Iroise will be weak and more across the track than opposing it.

Passing through the Raz itself is fairly straightforward by day. The main difficulty lies in finding the smoothest water. This tends to be towards the Ile de Sein side of the channel. On a southbound passage, from a point midway between Tevennec and Basse Jeaune make for Le Chat on a bearing of 220° until Tevennic bears 330° astern. Round La Plate about half a mile off, holding this heading until the Vieille light bears due north. If the overfalls are bad, a quicker escape from them can be made by cutting inshore towards Pointe Koummoudog soon after passing La Plate, holding an offing of about half a mile from the cliffs. On the Ile de Sein side beware Kornog Bras, a shallow patch on which any southerly swell breaks heavily.

For a northward passage, once La Plate bears due north turn towards Tevennec on a bearing of 330°. The overfalls tend to start abeam of La Plate, stretching northwards for some way. To escape from the worst of them, turn towards the middle of Baie des Trépassés as soon as Pointe du Raz is open to the north of La Vieille lighthouse. Do not go too far into the bay, especially if continuing to harbours in the Baie de

Pointe de Toulinguet, en route from Camaret towards the Raz

Looking east from Ile de Sein anchorage at low water. Above half tide the anchorage is exposed to weather from this direction. In the distance is the Pointe du Raz

Douarnenez, as Cornoc Treas and Basse Nevez (both awash at low water) lie in your path on the north side of the bay. A clearing bearing of 160° on the semaphore on Pte du Raz will keep you out of their way.

The Raz is surrounded by powerful sectored lights and a passage at night is perfectly possible. What will not be possible is to judge the smoothest water in the dark. You will have to stick to the courses the lighthouses give you, and with a good grace take all that the sea throws at you out of the darkness. From the north, approach La Vieille (Oc(2+1)WRG.12s33m18-13M Horn (2+1)60s) in its white sector on a bearing of 180° until you enter the white sector of Le Chat (Fl(2)WRG.6s9-6M). Turn towards Le Chat, staying in its white sector until you enter the directional flashing sector of the Tevennec light (Q.WR.28m9/6M DirFl.4s24m12M). Stay in this sector until Le Chat turns green. You are now clear of the hazards of the Raz.

From the south, approach along the edge of the red sector of the Pointe de Lervily light visible astern. When you enter the flashing directional sector of the Tevennec light turn towards it and stay in this sector until Le Chat turns white. Leaving Le Chat astern, stay in this sector until you are in the northern white sector of La Vieille. Once north of a line between Tevennec and Basse Jeaune you are in clear water.

HARBOURS AND ANCHORAGES

Ile de Sein
48°02´N 04°51´W

At first sight the island seems to be surrounded by impenetrable reefs. In reality the entrance is well marked and not too difficult. There are two entrance channels. Chenal d'Ezaudi is the easiest to identify, being marked by the starboard-hand buoy Cornoc An Ar Braden (Fl.G.4s). From here identify the Men Brial lighthouse (Oc(2)WRG. 6s16m12-7M) and beyond it the third house from the left which is painted white with a black stripe down the wall. Approach with these in transit, or with the house not quite open to the left of the lighthouse. Leave the white North Beacon Tower well to port and leave the unlit starboard-hand beacon Guernic to starboard. In practice, the hazards close to this track show up, even when covered by breaking water over them from the almost ever-present swell. The Guernic beacon sits in the middle of the rock it marks, not on the near edge, so don't cut it too fine.

The harbour dries south of the Men Brial lighthouse. Unless able to take the ground, anchor north of this, clear of fishing boat moorings. The bottom is sand over rock. Shelter is good from the south round to the northwest. Below half tide the rocks to the east also give protection. The harbour is best avoided in winds from north through to southeast.

A fishing fleet uses Ile de Sein as a base, returning to the harbour in the evenings and drinking in the bars. In the daytime the island is busy with day trippers, coming ashore from the *vedettes*. Despite these two itinerant populations the island seems to retain a air of isolation and aloofness from the outside world.

Facilities

A few bars and small shops in the village. Repairs can be arranged but the marine services are more attuned to the needs of the fishing fleet. Water is a precious commodity on the island so it is best to make sure you bring enough on board.

Breaking swells mark a rock close to the Chenal d'Ezaudi, the northern entrance to Ile de Sein harbour

Camaret

48°17′N 04°35′W

Set in the southwestern corner of the Rade de Brest, Camaret is the base for what remains of the local *langoustier* fleet. The harbour is easy to enter and is well sheltered except from the northeast. The marina is protected by the northern breakwater but the visitors' moorings off the south side of the entrance can be subject to swell. Approaching around Pointe Grand Gouin the Tour Vaubin on the wall above the marina is easily identifiable from seaward. At night approach in the white sector of the light (Iso.WG.4s7m12/9M) on the breakwater end and beware of the presence of fish farm cages within the bay.

Facilities

The harbour is developing as a major yachting centre. Chandlery, engineers, repairers and sailmakers are all to be found close to the yacht berths. A large supermarket is a short distance from the harbour.

Morgat

48°13′0N 04°32′0W

This artificial harbour in the north side of the Baie de Douarnenez is the closest secure berth to the north of the Raz de Sein. Shelter is complete in the marina and hazards in the approach are easily avoided. The sea caves below the lighthouse are interesting to visit by dinghy.

Facilities

Small shops and bars are to be found near the excellent bathing beach. For more comprehensive shops the town of Crozon is 1½ miles away.

Audierne

48°00′.0N 04°33′.0W

Set at the mouth of the Goyen River, about 10 miles from the Raz, Audierne is an attractive little town. There are no hazards in the approach from the west but a reef, La Gamelle, sits in the middle of the bay. It is marked by two cardinal buoys, Gamelle Ouest, which is lit and

PIPER'S EXPERIENCE – RAZ DE SEIN

Piper and I had spent the night in Camaret, enjoying local *langoustines* which I helped down with a glass or two of Bordeaux and some fresh bread. The wind was northerly Force 2 and we left with plenty time in hand to make the Raz by slack water. I dropped the mooring and sailed off under headsail, hoisting the main as we made enough northing to round Pointe de Grand Gouin on the next tack. Gybing around Pointe Toulinguet we stayed close inshore and followed the Chenal de Toulinguet into open water. The wind was still light and just fine on the starboard quarter, and above me a seamless blue sky and ahead almost fifteen miles of gently undulating blue water. I spent the next fifteen minutes in concentrated activity, running lines to blocks, checking sheet and guy leads and fixing the height of the pole. When all was ready I hauled on the halyard and the spinnaker climbed up the mast. At first it lay inert, blanketed by the squared off main. A heave on the guy and the pole swung out, the sail filled and *Piper* accelerated. For the next two hours the only sound was the chuckle of water in her wake. The wind stayed steady and the autopilot steered an

unerringly straight line across the sea.

As we approached Basse Jeaune I let go the guy and the spinnaker collapsed round in the lee of the main. As I fed out the halyard I pulled in the sheet, gathering in the sail under the boom and stuffing it down the main hatch. It was a little while before slack water and the speed we lost was soon made up by the run of the tide. My mouth was dry in anticipation as La Plate drew near. Very soon La Plate and La Vieille were in line and then astern as we swept by in smooth blue water. We hit a little turbulence once through and followed the example of a French yacht, cutting inshore around the edge of the roughness. This was meant to be the last great obstacle on my way south. It was something of an anticlimax, but I wasn't complaining. Within two hours I was anchored peacefully in Ste Evette. Heading northwards we left Audierne under a grey sky, aiming to pass through the Raz at low-water slack. The wind was northwesterly, only Force 3 to 4 but under the glowering sky it felt stronger. We were close hauled all the way to the Raz but the sea was smooth in the lee of the cliffs, and *Piper* flew. Even so, by the time we got there the flood was just beginning to run. I did a quick mental calculation and reckoned that we were a few days yet from springs. As we

drew level with La Plate the rain started. I held the starboard tack, watching the waves sweep over the rocks as the La Vieille lighthouse crossed *Piper's* stern. The seas were mounting rapidly, short and steep with crests that were just beginning to curl. A yacht that had passed through ahead of us was bouncing wildly on a direct course northwards. I tacked *Piper* in towards Baie des Trépassés, sailing her very free and letting the tide do the windward work, glad that we had not been any later and relieved that it was no nearer springs. As we tucked into the bay the sea lost much of its venom. The northbound yacht, motorsailing with her main sheeted almost flat, continued to take a beating. I watched through binoculars as she hobby-horsed violently, throwing spray into the air. I could also see the boundary of the rough water, clearly defined on the surface. With some relief we cleared the hazards in the north of the bay and I swung *Piper* onto a broad reach for Douarnenez.

has a whistle, and the unlit Gamelle Est, which has a bell.

Entry to the river should only be made on a rising tide, preferably within two hours of high water. Entry should not be attempted in rough southerly weather. Space is limited in the marina and there are few berths for yachts over 9 metres.

The anchorage at Ste Evette is accessible at all states of the tide but is subject to swell in winds from a southerly quarter. Mooring buoys are provided (for which there is a charge) and there is a little room to anchor to the east of the moorings.

Facilities
In Audierne harbour repair services are available and there are nearby shops, supermarket, post office and banks. At Ste Evette there are bars, a restaurant and a few tourist shops. Fuel at the root of the pier.

Baie des Trepasses
48°02´.8N 04°43´.0W

Corpses thrown into the sea from Les Iles de Sein, where the soil is too thin for burials of the dead, were said to wash up in this bay on the north side of the Pointe du Raz. Anchor off the beautiful sandy beach to await a fair tide for a passage of the Raz.

In the north side of the bay Cornoc Treas dries 0.4m and Basse Nevez dries 0.1m. There are no facilities.

CHARTS AND PILOTS

Imray C36, C37
Admiralty 2351, 3427, 798
SHOM 7121, 7147
Secret Anchorages of Brittany Peter Cumberlidge (Imray)
North Biscay Mike and Gill Barron/RCC (Imray)

15. STRANGFORD LOUGH NARROWS

Strangford Lough is a beautiful area of almost landlocked water. Sleek dairy cattle graze in green fields sloping gently down to calm water. Trees and hedgerows are alive with birds and wild flowers. The quiet waterway offers complete shelter from the rough weather out in the Irish Sea. Ashore the pubs and yacht clubs are friendly and welcoming. This is a place to slow down and forget about the pace of life and the stormy weather in the world outside.

The lough covers an area about 12 miles from south to north and up to 3 miles from east to west. The spring tidal range is 3.2 metres at Strangford and the only entrance and exit for the water is through The Narrows, a five-mile channel opening to the sea between Ballyquintin Point and Killard Point. In places the channel is little more than 400 metres wide and tides can attain rates of 7.8 knots at springs. Fortunately for those passing this way, the channel is fairly straight, although depths do vary considerably from around 20 metres to almost 60 metres in places. Just north of Angus Rock the channel is at its shallowest, being charted at 2.3 metres. The Narrows are at their widest here, being divided by Angus Rock into the East and West Channels.

On the flood the worst turbulence is caused by the obstructions projecting from either shore, particularly between Gowland and the Black Islands. A rotary eddy is set up here, known as the Routen Wheel. As this flow enters the Lough the energy is dissipated in an area of impressive but harmless eddies and

Approaching the Irish coast as the sun beats down

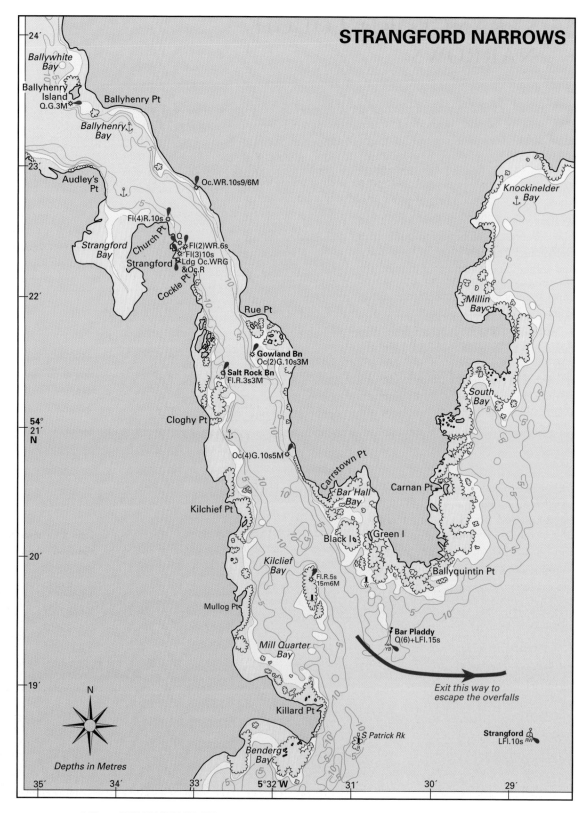

STRANGFORD NARROWS

24'

Ballywhite Bay

Ballyhenry Island
Q.G.3M

Ballyhenry Pt

Ballyhenry Bay

23'

Audley's Pt

Oc.WR.10s9/6M

Knockinelder Bay

Fl(4)R.10s

Church Pt
Q Q
Fl(2)WR.6s
Fl(3)10s
Strangford
Ldg Oc.WRG
&Oc.R

Strangford Bay

Cockle Pt

22'

Rue Pt

Millin Bay

Gowland Bn
Oc(2)G.10s3M

Salt Rock Bn
Fl.R.3s3M

South Bay

Cloghy Pt

**54°
21'
N**

Oc(4)G.10s5M

Carrstown Pt

Bar'Hall Bay

Carnan Pt

Kilchief Pt

Black I
Green I

20'

Kilchief Bay

Fl.R.5s
15m6M

Ballyquintin Pt

Mullog Pt

Bar Pladdy
Q(6)+LFl.15s
YB

Mill Quarter Bay

19'

N

Exit this way to escape the overfalls

Killard Pt

S Patrick Rk
R

Strangford
LFl.10s RW

Depths in Metres

Benderg Bay

35'   34'   33'   5°32'W   31'   30'   29'

minor whirlpools. Though the speed of the current can be alarming, entry is rarely hazardous.

On the ebb the water is often smooth at the inland end and there is turbulence within the channel downstream of obstructions. Around the shallows north of Angus Rock there can be turbulence but the sting is in the tail. The ebb, running past the Angus Rock at up to 7.5 knots flows straight out into the north-going ebb in the Irish Sea. In the presence of a southerly wind or swell this meeting can be extremely unpleasant, with overfalls extending almost two miles southeast from Bar Pladdy buoy. A large standing wave has been experienced extending right across the channel just north of Bar Pladdy.

The problem when leaving is that there will be no clue when you commit yourself at Portaferry as to the state of the sea at the bar, and though you may want to turn back on seeing breaking seas ahead there will be no escaping the inevitable.

GETTING IN

This is a low-lying coast with small hills which all seem similar. With few buildings and no dramatic headlands, identifying the entrance from seaward can be difficult. A great help is the line drawing along the left-hand edge of chart

2156, a masterpiece of the cartographer's art. Approaching from the northwest, Quintin Rock (dries 0.3) is a hazard. A transit through Patrick's Rock, marked by a red perch, and the white obelisk at the south end of Gunn's island is marked on the chart. Staying southeast of this will keep you clear.

In a sailing yacht a passage of the five-mile channel of The Narrows is only possible with a fair tide, and though entry can be achieved safely at any time during the flood it is preferable near slack water. If entering on the last of the flood, allow enough time to be through The Narrows before the turn or it could spit you out again.

From the Bar Pladdy buoy identify Angus Rock (Fl.R.5s6M.) Its white tower is very conspicuous. The channel is marked by a series of transits (see plan). The first and most important is formed by the beacons off Dogtail Point

At the northern end of the Narrows the energy of the turbulence is dissipated in harmless but impressive eddies

Angus Rock ahead as *Piper* nears the Irish Sea

The tower on Angus Rock

(Oc(4)G.10s2m5M) a mile beyond Angus Rock and Gowland (Oc(2)G.10s6m5M) ¾ mile beyond this on a bearingof 341°. In practice, by day these are difficult to spot and they are most useful at night.

There is ample depth throughout the length of the Narrows and all the hazards are well marked and close to the shore. It is sufficient, therefore, having left Angus Rock about a cable to port, to stay in mid-channel from Carrstown Point and count off the beacons on the shore until the Lough opens before you.

GETTING OUT

If leaving to head northwards be in position stemming the tide off Portaferry just before high water. This will allow you to take full advantage of the northgoing ebb in the Irish Sea and the ebb will have been running for not much more than

The entrance to the narrow creek that is home to the Down Cruising Club. The lightship clubhouse is just appearing

half an hour by the time you reach the Bar. On passing Angus Rock either use the Gowland-Dogtail Point leading line astern, or, more easily, make for a point about midway between Bar Pladdy Buoy and St Patrick's Rock. Once Bar Pladdy Buoy bears due east turn to round it before laying a course towards South Rock lightship. If there are overfalls this course will avoid the worst of them and have you out of their way in the shortest possible time.

Leaving to head southwards take the last hour of the ebb, arriving at the bar at or just before low water. In the presence of southerly wind or swell the overfalls should not have developed. A southerly course from the bar would take you through the roughest of the area of overfalls. If it is necessary to avoid them, turn eastwards around Bar Pladdy buoy, standing offshore until clear of the Strangford Safe Water buoy (L Fl. 10s Whis.) before turning southwards.

Tides
Killard Point = HW Dover
The Narrows and Strangford Lough
Dover +0140

	MHWS	MHWN	MLWN	MLWS
Killard Point				
	4.4	3.8	1.2	0.5
Strangford				
	3.6	3.1	0.9	0.4

HARBOUR INFORMATION

Portaferry
54°22′.7N 05°33′.0W

The small marina is set out of the main run of the tide near the inner end of the narrows. Entry is complicated by the strength of the tide off the entrance and the narrowness of the entrance channel. The flow within the pontoons can be a help with berthing, or not, and it is essential to use effective spring lines when tying up. Showers and toilets are located in the Barholm Hostel. Diesel is

available at the Slip Inn, just across the road from the head of the slipway. north of the marina is the ferry slip for the small car ferry between here and Strangford village, just diagonally across the narrows.

Portaferry itself is a pleasant little town, popular with holiday makers. There are banks, shops and a post office and a good selection of pubs and eating places. The fish and chip shop is in the finest tradition of British fish and chips - none of your skinny 'fries' here. To find it, walk up Ferry Street and follow your nose.

Contact
Portaferry Marina
VHF M2, 80. ☎ 028 42 729598

Piper **on a mooring at Quoyle. The yacht club is very friendly and welcoming, as are they all in the Lough**

From the slip in Strangford Bay, looking across the water to Portaferry

PIPER'S EXPERIENCE STRANGFORD LOUGH NARROWS

Inward

The sea was as smooth as glass. The sun beat down, hot on deck, hot below. The drinking water was tepid and tasted of sterilising fluid. For the past hour I'd been trailing a bottle of beer over the side on about twenty metres of line. At our speed of just over two knots, the angle of its line indicated that it was in the cool depths of at least ten metres. I decided it was time. It was my last bottle. I pulled in my treasure, opener at the ready. There seemed to be more weight on the line than just one bottle of beer and as it neared the surface I could see that some seaweed had wrapped itself around the line and the neck of its precious cargo. I lifted the weed-laden bottle clear of the water and gave the line a little shake to dislodge the weed. The line went suddenly slack and with a splash weed and bottle returned to the depths. I watched in disapointment as its sinking form fell slowly astern.

Ah, well. . . !

Away to the south the conical forms of the Mountains of Mourne showed grey against the golden light. The coastline was low and I constantly compared the shapes ahead with the drawing along the edge of my Admiralty chart. Due north of *Piper's* position the South Rock lightship was unmistakable at least, but was that Tara Hill? At last I got a set of bearings that made sense. Now confident of my position I laid off a course to pass half a mile southeast of Ballyquintin Point. Decision made, I sneaked a peep at the GPS, kept out of sight since I'd left the Isle of Man. It told me what I already knew and I immediately felt as if I'd cheated in my game of 'What if Mr Clinton turns it off?' Despite the light winds that had plagued my passage the timing was perfect. The last of the ebb was just creeping out of the channel as we approached the Bar Pladdy buoy. The wind had now died completely and the engine swung *Piper* round to meet the current.

I have sailed the Irish Sea for twenty years or so but this was the first time I had visited Strangford Lough. I have been regaled with horror stories of its entrance channel, tales of overfalls and whirlpools to chill the blood. Perhaps these had put me off. Perhaps I'd always been going somewhere else and just never got around to it. Either way, I was about to find out for myself. Bar Pladdy was astern and to port the sun was sinking towards the black silhouette of Kilclief Castle.

The light was low and golden as I tried to judge my distance off from the Angus Rock. Its tower raised a warning finger. I tried to spot the transit marks but all detail in that direction was lost in the dazzle. Giving it up, we swept by the rock a cable off by eye. To starboard the fields were green, bathed in the warmth of a perfect summer's evening. I had no difficulty identifying the beacon off Dogtail Point and after that the Gowland Beacon as we passed, seeing them with the light now over my shoulder. Ahead, a ribbon of smooth water led us towards the inland waterway of Strangford Lough. In this light the transits were impossible but the hazards on either hand were easy to spot and Salt Rock and Rue Point were passed without mishap.

By now the pace of the current was accelerating noticeably as the tide got into its stride. The patchwork of fields passed quickly to right and left and soon I could see the pontoons of Portaferry marina. The entrance buoys are quite small and, staking all on the hope that I'd got it right, I motored briskly across the flow and aimed *Piper* at the small gap. The depth reduced to around 3m as we entered the little bay and swung round the pontoon. There was only one vacant berth and I tucked *Piper* into it using the weaker flow through the pontoons to ferry glide into position, lines and fenders at the ready. Willing hands ashore held her steady until I had her secured and in a few minutes I could relax.

The light was almost gone as I walked ashore for a shower and a drink to wash away some of the heat of the day. I managed the shower in the hostel, which also houses the marina office, but pubs close early on Sunday evenings in the Province so I had to content myself with a can of a well-known fizzy drink to go with my fish and chips. Next morning I went in search of diesel and was directed to ask at the Slip Inn pub. I thought this was a joke and had a mental picture of red diesel being pulled from a pump at the bar. Still unsure, I turned up at the Slip Inn with my jerry cans. It felt very strange ordering 'a pint of Guinness and four gallons of diesel please', but both my glass and my jerry cans were duly filled. For the next few days I cruised gently around in perfect security, photographed Princess Anne, had a memorable night in the Down Cruising Club's lightship clubhouse and met some very friendly and wonderfully hospitable people.

Outward

As I steered *Piper* towards the open water of the Irish Sea I felt more than a hint of regret at having left it so long to make my first visit to this lovely place. I had spent only a short time in this exquisite inland sea, but now it was time to go. During the passage into Strangford Lough the entrance plainly had the subdued power of a sleeping tiger but as with all these things, the trick is to catch the tiger asleep.

The spring ebb was already running when I left Portaferry. In the Lough the water was smooth but the swaying treetops would have provided a clue for the observant. As we approached Rue Point a short chop buffeted *Piper*'s stem. South of the point the turbulence of the Routen Wheel was unnerving and I had to respond quickly as an unseen hand pushed *Piper* off course. With every inch towards the sea conditions seemed worse. Then after we passed between Gowland and the Salt Rock things calmed down, although still choppy with eddies pushing this way and that. The tower of Angus

Rock stood out against the sea horizon between Ballyquintin and Killard Points. The islet swept up swiftly and was soon astern.

Firmly in the grip of the tide, *Piper* charged on, our speed over the ground over ten knots. She plunged into increasing seas and I scanned ahead for the Bar Pladdy buoy through the spray flying aft. I spotted it at last and swung *Piper* onto an eastward course as soon as we were clear outside Quintin rock. With Ballyquintin astern the seas diminished rapidly and with *Piper* on a broad reach towards the South Rock lightship and a fair tide under us the shaking was forgotten before the decks had dried.

Strangford Bay: leafy solitude

Ardglass

54°15´.6N 05°36´.0W

Once a small fishing harbour with little room for yachts, the development of the marina has made Ardglass a very useful stopover from which to time an entrance to Strangford Lough. There are 30 visitors' berths and a least depth of 1.7m in the marina. There is a supermarket on the quay, power and water alongside, showers, toilets and laundry facilities.

Contact

Phennick Cove Marina
VHF 37, 80. ☎ 028 44 842 332

Strangford Lough Yacht Club

Striped fields reflecting in the water of Ringhaddy Sound

CHARTS AND PILOTS

Imray C62
Admiralty 2156 is essential
East and North Coasts of Ireland (Irish Cruising Club Sailing Directions)

16. THE SWELLIES

Slack water lasts for a few minutes, then the tide starts to run. As the rate builds up the surface of the water swirls and foams. In places standing waves or hollows form as the water forces itself over an underwater obstruction. In the middle of the flood, water south of the Britannia Bridge is visibly higher than on the other side and pours down in a low waterfall between the Cribbin Rock and the island of Gored Goch with its white cottage, all the while emitting a low roar. White water marks every rock, giving the appearance more of a river in spate rather than the sea. At the bend, by the Swelly Rock, the rate is at its maximum (ten knots at springs) and a bow wave forms around the beacon. The flood rushes on toward the Menai Bridge, foaming over the Platters before passing under the span to continue swiftly but more peacefully up the Menai Strait to rejoin the Irish Sea. This is the Swellies.

The Isle of Anglesey lies at the northwestern corner of Wales, separated from the mainland by a narrow strip of water, the Menai Strait. The island, in Welsh Ynys Mon, is roughly twenty miles square and stands right in the way of the tide, which floods up the St George's Channel into the Irish Sea. Tides in the

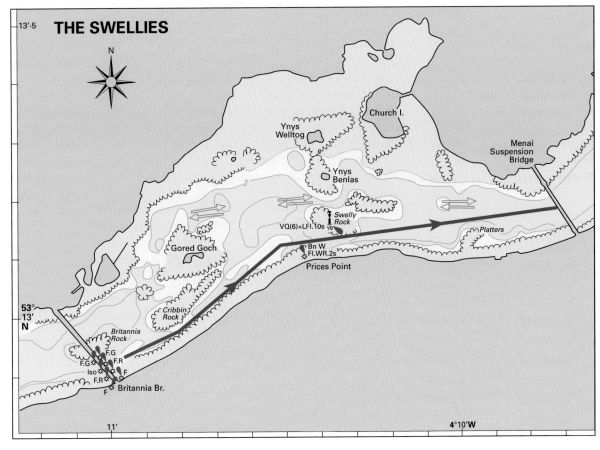

The Swellies from Britannia Bridge. The ebb has just started to run

Irish Sea are strong and when this mass of water reaches the north of Anglesey it swings through ninety degrees to the east to flow into Liverpool Bay. The turbulence produced by the sudden change of direction creates impressive overfalls at the North and South Stacks and at the Skerries, with standing waves between Carmel Head and West Mouse. These waters are dangerous and must be treated with respect, but the Fearsome Reputation goes to a short stretch of water within the Menai Strait, the Swellies.

At the narrowest point of the Strait the channel 'between the bridges' is braided with rocks and obstructions. From either end of the Strait to each bridge, the tide has a swift but relatively smooth passage. In the Swellies, the narrowness of the channel and the nature of the bottom seem designed to create

turmoil. And yet boats do pass routinely through this maelstrom, most of them without incident. Is the reputation of the Swellies undeserved, or is there something else?

As with many things, the secret of the Swellies is timing. At the right time and in the right conditions the Swellies passage is just a straightforward piece of pilotage. Alan Hollingworth has sailed in the Menai Strait for many years and says: *'If you stick to the right time it's not a problem. I suppose because we go through so often we forget the reputation the Swellies has.'*

WHEN TO GO THROUGH

The tide dominates all waterborne activity in the Menai Strait and the state of the tide is a constant point of reference for all involved with the sea. Spend a day on a mooring in the Strait and you will see a sudden flurry of activity as several boats pass by, though all was quiet before. A local sailor may just raise an eye to watch them and think 'Swellies slack'. You may see one yacht pass down alone toward the bridge. Suddenly, moorings are being dropped and yachts are getting under way as one after another they follow in her wake. It's as if no-one wants to be first. Even with the local sailors, the Swellies commands respect.

Without detailed local knowledge and a depth of experience the only safe time to pass through is at slack water, which is of very short duration.

The key time for the Swellies is **two hours before Liverpool high water**. (For some reason, perhaps because two hours is easy to remember, local sailors always relate Swellies slack to Liverpool.)

The passage is just under 1.5 miles, so the average cruising yacht should be through in about twenty minutes.

Gored Goch as we pass through the Swellies at 'slack' water

Gored Goch

The beacon on the
Swelly Rock

Heading southwest

The ebb starts first at the south of the Strait. If you want to pass out over Caernarfon Bar it is best to be away promptly but until the flood eases it is impossible to go under the Menai Bridge against the flow.

Using Liverpool –0200 as the benchmark, aim to pass under the bridge about 15 minutes early, meeting the last of the flood. You will then avoid being swept along at a rate faster than you would like if working out the passage for the first time. Using this timing you will pick up the ebb near Plas Newydd, just south of the Britannia Bridge.

Heading northeast

If making the passage for the first time it is wisest to stick close to the slack-water benchmark, but you must avoid being late as the tide will turn against you with the force and suddenness of someone throwing a switch. If you are confident that you know the way, passing through up to 45mins early has the advantage of giving you a fair tide all the way up to Beaumaris. It will be an exciting ride as you watch the water swirling through the other span and off the medieval fish traps

around the island. It needs a quick hand on the helm to correct as the eddies throw your bow off first one way then the other. The alternative is to bash most of the way up the Strait with the ebb running against you at two to three knots.

Low-water slack

A passage at low-water slack is sometimes possible, preferably nearer neaps than springs. A study of the plan in the Admiralty chart will reveal several spots where depth at LAT is below 1m and just how narrow the channel is alongside the Cribbin Rock. A low-water passage requires extreme caution. The question I ask myself is 'how badly do I want to avoid waiting for high water slack?'

Of course, tidal predictions are no more than that: predictions. So the times may vary depending on weather conditions locally or even elsewhere in the Irish Sea.

PILOTAGE

Southwest

From Menai Bridge pass under the middle of the span of the bridge and make for the flagstaff in front of the gable of the white cottage on the island of Gored Goch. Between Price Point and the Swelly beacon stay parallel to the shore until you can see the SE end of the Britannia Bridge. Under the bridge, close to the shore are two white lattice beacons, sometimes hard to see through the gloom and greenery. These give a transit (051°/231°) to clear the Cribbin Rock. Stay on this line until abeam of the white pyramid beacon on the shore then turn to pass through the mid span of the mainland arch of the bridge. Once clear of the bridge turn towards the Anglesey shore to avoid a shallow patch.

Northeast

This is an exact reversal of the south west passage. Approaching the Britannia Bridge from mid-channel pass under the mid span of the mainland arch. Stay parallel to the shore until abeam of the white pyramid beacon then align the white lattice beacons astern. Off Price Point turn parallel to the shore until abeam of the Swelly Rock beacon then make for the mid span of the Menai Suspension Bridge. A red beacon on the shore beyond the bridge will give a transit with mid span to avoid being set across onto the Platters.

At night: The Swellies is well provided with lit navigation marks and, though scary, is not too difficult at night. Port and starboard lights are fixed to both sides of the Britannia Bridge. The pyramid beacon is not lit but shows up quite well in the ambient light. The transit beacons are lit and their flashing white lights are easier to pick out than in daylight. Passing between the Swelly Rock (Q6+LFl) and Price Point (WR.2s) the Menai Suspension Bridge comes into view. Identifying mid span is easy as the whole bridge is floodlit at night.

By giving the Swellies the respect they deserve, hundreds of craft of all sizes go through each year without mishap, but the Swellies has claimed a few victims. Every summer Beaumaris ILB answers a number of calls to small boats in distress, most often aground on either the Platters or the Cribbin Rock. Occasionally a sailing dinghy off Menai Bridge will lose the wind in the shelter of the high sides of the Strait and drift helplessly backwards beneath the Menai Bridge. When clubs are racing there is always a

Approaching the Swelly Rock heading NE. The Menai bridge is in view ahead

Price Point. The yacht is cutting a bit close to the Platters for comfort

Price's Point beacon

Once past the Swelly Rock line up the transit marks, lattice beacons under the mainland end of the Britannia

rescue boat on hand with the speed and power to pull them to safety.

In 1954 the naval sailing ship *HMS Conway*, retired and in use as a floating school, was to be towed through the Swellies. Before she cleared the Menai Bridge the tide turned against her, the towrope broke and she was swept down onto the Platters.

ANGLESEY TIDES

The tides around Anglesey that make the Swellies what it is are very complex. The flood, running up St George's Channel, arrives in Caernarfon Bay and some of it begins to flow into the southwestern end of the Menai Strait. Meanwhile, the bulk of the tide continues up the west side of Anglesey, arriving off the northeastern end of the Strait having travelled almost forty miles further. The result is a shifting balance, with water flowing into the Strait sometimes from one end, sometimes from both and with slack

A lot of traffic passes during the brief spell of slack water

Heading north it is possible to pass through early. The eddies and turbulence require a quick hand on the helm but you will carry a fair tide up the Strait

The Swellies at low, but not slack, water from the Menai Bridge

water occurring wherever the two flows meet with equal force. It is important to remember that slack water in the Menai Strait is not the same as high or low-water. Depending on where you are in the Strait the tide can be slack and falling, or going southwest, the direction of the ebb, and still rising or vice versa. (The terms 'high-water slack' and 'low-water slack' do not mean slack at high or low-water but are a convenient label for the period of slack water nearest the respective level of tide.)

THE LONGEST NAME

The village of Llanfairpwllgwyngyll-gogerychwyndrobwllllantysiliogogogoch overlooks the Swellies. The name, usually shortened to LlanfairPG, means 'The church of St Mary in a hollow of white hazel near a rapid whirlpool and near St Tysilio's church by the red cave.' The rapid whirlpool referred to in the name is the Swellies. I was disappointed to learn that the longest place name in Britain was actually coined in the nineteenth century with the aim of attracting tourists to Anglesey.

THE HARBOURS

Port Dinorwic
53°11´.2N 04°12´.6W

Approaching by road there is no sign towards Port Dinorwic. Instead, road signs now bear the older name of Y Felinheli, a change largely ignored in most conversations. The cleft in the mainland shore that shelters Vaynol Dock has been used as a harbour for thousands of years: the Romans had a dock here. The present dock with its lock gates was originally built to serve the slate quarries

PIPER'S EXPERIENCE THE SWELLIES

Piper has passed through the Swellies on countless occasions. (Her mooring is only a mile or so north of the Menai Bridge.) A northward passage is the end to most of my voyages and is always an emotional time. Returning from Norway via the Baltic, Holland and the English Channel we had crossed the Bar just before dawn and the early mist was still haunting the water as we passed under the Britannia Bridge. A heron fished from the shore beside the pyramid beacon. I thought, 'If he's lucky he'll have sea bass for breakfast.' Off Menai Bridge the first familiar faces in 4,000 miles waved a greeting: it was Ralph and Trish Morris aboard *Trilogy*, preparing to go the other way.

'Welcome home. Good trip?'. Sometimes I think that coming home is the best reason for going away.

On one occasion *Piper* nearly went through the Swellies unintentionally. We had just filled up with water at Menai Bridge Pier and had swung out into the channel to motor against the tide up to the Gazelle Hotel, an excellent place for lunch. There was not a breath of wind and, aware of our dependence on the motor, I seemed to sense that it was faltering. No sooner had we

cleared the moorings off the pier than the engine stopped. The silence was deafening. I tried the starter. The exhaust made the odd bronchitic cough but refused to restart. Having changed the fuel filter that morning, I suspected air in the line. All I needed was a couple of minutes to locate the problem and get the engine restarted, but according to habit neither time nor tide were going to wait. Perhaps I could drift down onto a free mooring or alongside a moored yacht to buy some precious minutes; but there was nothing within reach and, besides, approaching another yacht without control at a closing speed of 3 knots would certainly result in damage to both.

I judged that our drift would take us under the Menai Bridge, close to the Anglesey shore so we'd miss the Platters, but what about the Swelly Rock?

Just then a yacht pulled away from one of the moorings. I grabbed a heaving line from a cockpit locker and walked up forward. As I did so I shouted over to them and waved my tow rope. My would-be rescuers appraised the situation immediately, swung skilfully across the tide and passed close alongside *Piper*, catching the end of the line and taking in the slack to keep their propeller clear. As we all drifted down towards the bridge they edged away,

keeping the line taut until both yachts were moving in concert. Their skipper explained that he couldn't tow me for long because his engine was struggling and he was afraid it would overheat, but not far upstream was a vacant mooring. He swung across the tide, *Piper* following like a reluctant puppy, and as the mooring buoy passed beneath her stem I got the boathook into its ring. With the pick-up buoy aboard, the tow was dropped and *Piper* was safe. It took two or three minutes to bleed the fuel line and the motor was running sweetly again. I was still in time for a relaxed lunch in front of the Gazelle Hotel. As I ate I reflected on how different my position would have been if not for some timely, skilful and generous assistance.

The island of Gored Goch through the Britannia Bridge from the southwest

The Menai Bridge and the Swellies at near low water

in the mountains. Now it provides completely sheltered berths for yachts. Approach the lock close along the south wall, where there is a fuelling berth. The tidal dock, southwest of the lock entrance, has no spaces for visitors. Limited depth is maintained by a sill which dries. A tide gauge is fixed to the wall.

The lock gates open on request approximately HW±0230. Call Dinorwic Marina on VHF Ch 37. ☎ 01248 671500.

Most of the moorings in the bay are private but off the entrance to the lock there are visitors' moorings owned by Port Dinorwic Yacht Harbour.

Facilities

Showers, toilets and laundry. Diesel alongside outside the lock gate, HW±0300 Contact the marina office.

Engineers, repairs, 16-ton travel-hoist at Dinas Boatyard at the south side of the bay. ☎ 01248 671642

There is a small shop/off-licence on the main street of Y Filinheli. The Gardd Ffon pub serves food.

Menai Bridge
53°13´.6N 04°9´.2W

It is sometimes possible to lie alongside Menai Bridge pier when the research vessel *Prince Madog* does not need the berth. Permission can be obtained from the harbourmaster. When approaching the pier at low speed many yachts are caught out by the reverse eddy which runs close to the pier.

There is water alongside at the pier. Ashore the Liverpool Arms serves good food and there is a range of small shops in the town including banks, post office,

Camping Gaz and Calor Gas refills. There is a landing for dinghies at the Gazelle Hotel, 2 miles northeast. The hotel serves good food and overlooks the water. If using the private moorings for a short lunch stop, exercise due courtesy to their owners. Anchoring is inadvisable due to the amount of old chain and debris on the bottom.

Contact
Menai Bridge Piermaster:
☎ 01248 712312

Beaumaris
53°1′5′.6N 04°5′.4W

Apart from a small number of yellow visitors' moorings between Menai Bridge and Beaumaris there are few visitors'' berths available. There is an anchorage in The Pool, to the southeast of the port-hand buoy B10 off Beaumaris Pier. It may be possible to use a private mooring by prior arrangement or for a short period so long as the yacht is not left unattended. The spit between B10 and B12 dries and seems to be a popular low-water scrubbing berth.

Ashore in Beaumaris town there is a range of small shops, pubs and cafés. On Gallows Point at the southern end of Beaumaris Bay the North West Venturers Yacht Club welcomes visiting yacht crews to use its showers and toilets. Water from tap in front of clubhouse. Anglesey Boat Company has repair facilities and chandlery.

Contacts
ABC ☎ 10248 811413
NWVYC ☎ 01248 810023

CHARTS AND PILOTS

Imray C61 St Georges Channel has a small plan of the Swellies.
Admiralty 1464
Cruising Anglesey and Adjoining Waters Ralph Morris (Imray). Has clear plans and directions including an hour-by-hour tidal atlas for the Menai Strait.

Approaching the Menai Bridge from the direction of Menai Bridge Pier. Britannia Bridge is visible. In between is the Swellies

INDEX